THE BOOMER'S
ULTIMATE GUIDE TO

Social Media Marketing

THE BOOMER'S ULTIMATE GUIDE TO

Social Media Marketing

Learn How to Navigate the Digital Highway

Kalynn Amadio

MAVEN HOUSE

Published by Maven House Press, 4 Snead Ct., Palmyra, VA 22963
610.883.7988, www.mavenhousepress.com, info@mavenhousepress.com

Special discounts on bulk quantities of Maven House Press books are available to corporations, professional associations, and other organizations. For details contact the publisher.

While this publication is designed to provide accurate and authoritative information in regard to the subject matter covered, it is sold with the understanding that the publisher is not engaged in rendering legal, accounting, or other professional service. If legal advice or other expert assistance is required, the services of a competent professional person should be sought. — From the Declaration of Principles jointly adopted by a Committee of the American Bar Association and a Committee of Publishers and Associations

Library of Congress Control Number: 2015915548

Paperback ISBN: 978-1-938548-48-2
ePUB ISBN: 978-1-938548-49-4
ePDF ISBN: 978-1-938548-50-5
Kindle ISBN: 978-1-938548-61-1

Printed in the United States of America.

10 9 8 7 6 5 4 3 2 1

DEDICATION

♦ ♦ ♦ ♦ ♦

For my wonderful husband Damon,
who has always believed in me . . .
even when I stop believing in myself.

CONTENTS

♦ ♦ ♦ ♦ ♦

ACKNOWLEDGEMENTS

◆ ◆ ◆ ◆ ◆

WHO KNEW THAT A SUMMER PROJECT could turn into a nearly three-year odyssey? I literally went about getting published half-assed backwards, but that's another story! I would be remiss not to thank the people who helped me get to this lifetime goal of becoming a published author.

A heartfelt thanks to my Mind Trust group: Jean Caton, Christine Clifton, Marty Marsh, Ally Piper, and Claudia Sandman, who encouraged me, read the first draft, and gave critical feedback that kept me moving forward. I am humbled by your belief in me. "Don't think, just do!"

My appreciation for a great client and friend, David Rubin, who also read the first draft, took notes, and sat me down to share his insights.

Thanks to my editor, Jennifer Wilkov, who worked through every word, comma, and phrase. She helped me develop the material into something better. Then when a self-publishing summer project became something more, she edited my proposal to make it shine.

Thanks to the publicity goddess Jill Lublin who came on my podcast as a guest, then took me on as a client. She helped me form fundamental publicity strategies and presented my book idea to agents and publishers at Book Expo America. She and her partner Randy Peyser are how I connected with Maven House Press.

Thanks to Jim Pennypacker of Maven House, who believed in my idea enough to want to publish it. I can now cross one more thing off my bucket list.

As a local business owner, I spend a lot of time networking and have belonged to various networking groups over the years. My BNI (Business Networking International) group has been very supportive of this project, even to the point of helping me pick out the book cover. Thanks Network One . . . "Givers Gain!"

A big honey badger thank you to the graphic goddess J. Teri Elefante who has helped me with The Boomer Gal and ACT LOCAL Marketing for Small Business branding efforts. She is a true genius and great friend. If you need graphics, you need Teri at Absolute Perfection Graphics & Design.

Finally, thanks to my Mom and Dad, the best role models a kid could ever have. Thank you for letting me finish this book at your kitchen table. I love you.

How This Book Is Organized

THIS BOOK IS WRITTEN as a travel guide. Your approach to using it will be similar to planning a trip somewhere you've never been before – in this case to the world of social media marketing. The book is designed to help you develop a personalized MAP (Marketing Action Plan) that will guide you in making social media a useful and productive part of marketing your business. To help you plan your trip I've divided the book into four sections:

Introduction: Plan Your Trip is an introduction to social media marketing and defines the problem for boomer business professionals today – the world has changed and the new reality of social media means learning how to use a new marketing and communication tool. You will also see a list of the top ten social media websites (or platforms) in use today and the three best itineraries for baby boomer business owners.

Part One: Discover Social Media begins to build your foundation – why social media marketing is important and

how it works. It provides you with a framework for learning the steps necessary to create a successful social media
strategy. Examples of small businesses that successfully use
social media will fill out this framework. Finally, this section
describes the six most important social media destinations
for boomer business: Facebook, Twitter, LinkedIn, Pinterest,
Google Plus, and YouTube. You'll learn about their histories
and highlights so you'll be familiar with each destination before visiting.

Part Two: Your Survival Guide covers the how-to of
social media marketing including what you need to know
about social media language, etiquette, transport, frequency,
and metrics. Every social media website has its own language
and etiquette that you need to learn so you can communicate
better. There are several methods and tools available to deliver your content (words, images, audio, and video). You'll also
discover some frequency of delivery metrics to track return
on investment.

Part Three: Appendices includes step-by-step instructions on how to set up your social media accounts, profiles,
pages, and images and other detailed information relevant
to each of the six destinations covered in the guide. When
you're ready to detail your MAP to begin your journey, you'll
find references and extra resources available online listed in
this section.

Like any good guide, this book offers vital information about
each destination. Plan the perfect trip with advice from local
experts. Get ideas to make planning your itineraries easy and
discover lists of must-do experiences that are sure to become
favorite highlights.

Other Features of Note

Symbols. Throughout the guide you'll find key symbols to highlight information you shouldn't miss:

⭐ **Don't Miss** – gives you context to help make information meaningful or highlights something you may not have been aware of.

☞ **Local Knowledge** – has detailed action items to support you in using the information provided, as if you're already a longtime resident of the area.

⊗ **Hazard Zone** – indicates mistakes people tend to make. This is also a good place to stop and check that you have everything in order before continuing on your journey.

And There's More Online. What kind of digital marketing maven would I be if I didn't provide you with extra resources you can download? The goal is to help you make social media marketing achievable. To reach that goal, I've developed worksheets and checklists for you to use. You can access them from the website www.boomersultimateguidebooks. com (that's a long address so take the shortcut: www.thebug-books.com). My only request is that you share your name and email address with me, and I will do the same. You can email me with questions, comments, or just to say howdy right here: ka@thebugbooks.com.

Now read on, my friend. You're about to embark on a 21st century journey of marketing and communication. Discover social media and experience the best of online marketing. Bon voyage!

INTRODUCTION

• • • • •

Plan Your Trip

All journeys have secret destinations of which the traveler is unaware.

~ Martin Buber

I F YOU WERE BORN between 1946 and 1964 you have seen dramatic change in the world. One of the most startling changes is how we communicate. You probably walk around today with a phone in your pocket. Who could have imagined you would *never* be disconnected from the outside world?

This is Social Media

Since the World Wide Web (WWW) first arrived in the 1990s, we've been busy establishing ways to use it to interact socially. Being social is in our nature. Every new communication tool, from the Pony Express and telegraph to email and text messaging, is used to reach out and make connections, build relationships, and be social.

There's a parallel world out there. It's moving and changing, and you experience this world through digital media and the Internet. It's a virtual world that has dramatically altered how we speak to one another, day in and day out, through tools such as social media, video, and text messaging. The idea of using digital media to talk to friends, family, or colleagues is daunting. And even more daunting, now you must determine how to effectively use these methods of communication in your business.

Social media in particular seems to be the source of much confusion. There's an overwhelming number of websites to explore and track, each one having its own list of rules to follow and language to learn. Becoming successful with social media can help grow a thriving business, and understanding which websites to go to and how to behave once you get there can make all the difference.

Social Media's Top 10 Highlights

Here is a list of the top ten English-speaking social media websites in use today.[1]

1. **Facebook:** A social networking service founded by Mark Zuckerberg in 2004. Facebook's mission is to give people the power to share and make the world more open and connected. www.facebook.com

2. **Twitter:** A social networking and microblogging (short message) service invented in 2006 by Odeo. Twitter's mission is to give everyone the power to instantly create and share ideas and information, without barriers. www.twitter.com

③ **LinkedIn:** A social networking service launched in 2003. LinkedIn's mission is to connect the world's professionals to make them more productive and successful. www.linkedin.com

④ **Pinterest:** A visual discovery social networking service launched in 2010. "Pinterest is a place to discover ideas for all your projects and interests, handpicked by people like you." The platform is based on sharing and organizing images. www.pinterest.com

⑤ **Google Plus:** A social networking service launched in 2011 by Google. Google Plus is a platform for discovering and sharing digital content with friends, family, and coworkers. It's integrated with many other Google services and YouTube. www.plus.google.com

⑥ **Tumblr:** A microblogging and social networking service founded in 2007. Tumblr allows creative users to post short-form content in multimedia formats. www.tumblr.com

⑦ **Instagram:** A mobile photo- and video-sharing, social networking service launched in 2010. Instagram allows users to share and alter photos and videos on their platform and connect to other social networking services such as Facebook, Twitter, and Tumblr. Facebook purchased Instagram in 2012. www.instagram.com

⑧ **Flickr:** An image- and video-hosting service created in 2004. On Flickr, users share and explore photos and videos, and bloggers host images that they can embed (a term used for the insertion of content) in their blogs and on social media. www.flickr.com

⑨ **MySpace:** A social networking service with a strong music emphasis founded in 2003. MySpace is built to empower all artists – from musicians and designers to writers and photographers – to connect with audiences. www.myspace.com

⑩ **Meetup:** Social networking website launched in 2002 that facilitates offline group meetings. Groups are created based on common interests and can be searched by location. www.meetup.com

Social Media's Top Itineraries

Hundreds of active social media networking websites, excluding dating websites, are used by people all over the world to stay connected. With so many choices, how does a savvy baby boomer decide where to begin?

That's the purpose of this guide.

To get the most bang for the buck, we'll focus our attention on the six most popular social media sites for boomer business people. There are other sites frequented by twenty-somethings, and still others that appeal to thirty-somethings. We're going to begin our travels by visiting where consumers with income tend to hang out.

The six travel destinations we will explore are Facebook, Twitter, LinkedIn, Pinterest, Google Plus, and YouTube.

Here are the top three social media itineraries for baby boomer business owners to tour:

1 On The Street: This itinerary is a must for businesses that are primarily business-to-consumer oriented, also known as B2C. B2C businesses include storefronts, retail establishments, and service providers – such as attorneys, insurance agents, and financial planners – who deal directly with individual consumers. Restaurants and clothiers, hardware and sporting goods stores, residential realtors and dentists, any business that has offices at street level should plan on taking this trip. On The Street is a fun and friendly trip.

2 Enterprise: The Enterprise itinerary is for businesses that provide goods and services primarily to other businesses, known as B2B, rather than to the end consumer. Examples of business-to-business companies include manufacturers, wholesalers, and service providers that cater to businesses. The Enterprise trip will showcase how to position your company in the public eye even if the public at large may not understand what your business does. Unlike On The Street, the Enterprise trip is more subtle and suggestive and less showy.

3 Crossroads: The Crossroads itinerary captures the best of both worlds. It's for businesses that straddle B2C and B2B markets. It's also a great trip for those who are feeling current and modern or who are willing to risk becoming a celebrity in their marketplace. This trip is customizable to meet your needs. Whether you lean toward fun and flashy or understated and distinguished, a Crossroads trip can be the best time you've ever had online.

Changes in the Way We Communicate

It's well established that, because of technology and social media, the way we communicate is rapidly changing. Communication is now a constantly moving target of pervasive and non-linear interactions. A conversation that begins in one place can continue to a second and even a third before coming to an end. Keeping up with new ways of communicating requires a new and nimble skill set.

A perfect example of this is the way we communicate our marketing messages. Social media marketing is often thought of as advertising, but nothing could be further from the truth. Advertising is an example of what's called push communication. It's the kind of marketing that most baby boomers are familiar with. The marketing message is pushed out to potential customers, who passively receive information about the product or service and choose to buy or not based on that simple message. Social media marketing relies on what's called pull communication, where the marketing message pulls the potential customer, creating demand for the product or service. The distinction between push and pull is important because people believe only 14 percent of advertising.[2] Social media marketing, which relies on pull methods such as word-of-mouth (also known as social sharing) carries more weight in terms of converting a potential customer into a paying customer. In fact, social media has taken word-of-mouth to exponentially greater levels of importance. The resulting influence that social sharing has on your business is profound. Understanding this new way of communicating will be critical to your success.

Boomers have another communication dilemma to contend with – the Millennial Generation. Millennials communicate differently from boomers, and the difference in communication styles is vast. It's more important now than ever before to learn how to use all the resources and tools available to you to bridge that communication gap.

The New Communication Map

In 1883 Western Union declared, "The telephone is not a viable commercial product." We've had over 130 years of hindsight tell us that this type of thinking was an epic failure by Western Union. The belief that changing technology just goes away because we don't understand it won't fly. It's in

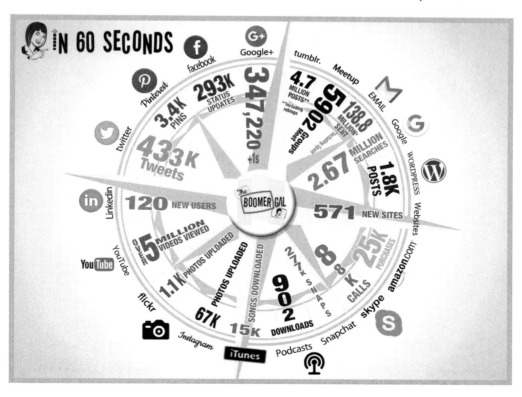

our nature to learn – to figure out how to better our world, including how to use technology to be more productive and better connected.

Here are some statistics that show you how important social media has become in connecting us (and the numbers are growing rapidly every year). In 2013 over 3 million companies had LinkedIn Company Pages. Google Plus added over 925,000 new users every day. More than 350 million photos were uploaded to Facebook daily. YouTube saw an astounding one hour of video uploaded every second.[3] According to Nielsen, 64 percent of U.S. adults use social media daily on a PC and a growing 47 percent use social media daily from their smartphone.[4]

Get Inspired

I'm a baby boomer, and I have to confess that, in the beginning, I hated the concept of social media. I couldn't fathom why anyone would want to waste time on Facebook or have conversations with total strangers using 140 characters at a time on Twitter. It didn't make sense to me – until I finally jumped on board and trekked into the heart of those websites. I've uncovered the value proposition that social media offers businesses, especially local businesses.

Social media is a way to get in front of ideal prospects, to increase customer retention and loyalty, and to grow *any* business. It's endlessly fun to use social media to build your business when you have the right guide showing you the way.

Imagine if you could generate more leads, become the go-to authority in your community, and have ideal prospects knocking on your door. It happens when prospects believe you're the only choice for them in your marketplace. What if all this were possible by spending only 34 minutes a day on social media?

What You Need to Know

Social media is the number one activity on the Internet, but not because social media is all about fun.[4] Remember, the Internet and social media are tools of communication. We communicate for pleasure, but we also connect with a purpose when it comes to business.

The explosion of social media happened because business people just like you discovered how to use it as part of a marketing strategy – to generate leads and build relationships with ideal prospects, donors, customers, or clients. The terminology we use or whether your business is for-profit or not-for-profit doesn't matter. You can reach the ideal people you want and need to reach to make your business a success.

The first step in using social media to generate growth and income for your business is to answer these questions:

- ◆ Where are my ideal prospects online?
- ◆ What should I talk about?
- ◆ How can I get noticed without wasting my time?
- ◆ Who is going to do all this extra work?
- ◆ When is it going to start making a difference to my business?

You have to know when, where, and how to streamline your efforts to get the most from your marketing dollars. You want results and you want to know how to grow your business without wasting your time online.

Everything you need to know is here in *The Boomer's Ultimate Guide to Social Media Marketing*, organized strategically so you end up with a personalized MAP (Marketing Action Plan) that will guide you in making social media a productive part of your business. Please don't spend another moment confused about how to generate leads, convert sales, or earn more money using social media. This guide will help you discover how to organize the chaos and think of social media as a tool, not an evil necessity or an obstacle to ignore.

PART ONE

Discover Social Media

CHAPTER ONE

◆ ◆ ◆ ◆ ◆

HIGHLIGHTS

Why Use Social Media?

You can have any color as long as it is black.

~ Henry Ford

GONE ARE THE DAYS when a business could tell the customer, "It's our way or the highway," as Henry Ford did. It's funny now, cute even, but if Ford were alive and running his business today with that mindset, he would fail, because the world has changed.

Social media is a worldwide phenomenon. Though young in the larger landscape of communication options, it has grown rapidly. It involves so many of us that you cannot ignore its existence and power in daily life.

You can still pick up the phone to have a conversation, but that phone is now smart. It can take messages and dictation, read your mail, and connect you to the Internet. Your phone can help you with directions, book restaurant reservations, find out what's playing at the movies, and help you buy tickets before you get to the theater. It can help you find the nearest, well, anything, and it's a bridge to all your social media ports of call.

I like statistics, so let me throw a few at you.

According to a study from Global Web Index (GWI), there were two key factors driving the social web in 2013.[1] The first factor was mobile – referring to that smartphone you carry or the tablet you use rather than your laptop computer. Use of a mobile device to access the Internet increased by 60.3 percent – to a whopping 818.4 million people – since 2011.

⭐ Smartphones account for 70 percent of the U.S. mobile phone market, and people spend more than 38 hours per month on their phones.[2] Americans who own smartphones or tablets spend over an hour daily on social media and browsing the Internet.[3,4]

The second factor was you – the boomers! Boomers, and more narrowly people 55–64 years old, are the fastest expanding demographic on Twitter, growing at a rate of 79 percent between Q2 2012 and Q1 2013. It's people 45–54 years old (the young boomers and their younger siblings) who contributed the fastest growth on both Facebook at 46 percent and Google Plus at 56 percent. If you're wondering whether your target markets – and perhaps your peers – are actually using social media, the answer is yes. Yes, they are.

Facebook joined the Fortune 500 list at number 482 in May of 2013.[5] That's a serious enterprise. In December of 2013 Facebook claimed over 757 million daily active users (DAU) and 556 million mobile DAUs.[6]

☛ A daily active user (DAU) is defined as someone who visits a social media page, views a post, or interacts with a post. This is different from registered users, which is the number of people who have a registered account but may not actively use it to visit the website. Social media sites such as Facebook keep statistics on visitors who access the site from a desktop computer versus visitors who access the site via mobile device or mobile app.

Twitter is the fastest growing social media site in the world according to GWI, with a growth rate of 44 percent from June 2012 to March 2013 and 288 million active users.[7] (It's also my favorite.)

If you are anything like me, you may still be in the habit of saying, "Put it in the VCR," when you really use a DVD or Blue Ray player. For Mother's Day, the hubby got me a new big-screen television. It's a Samsung Smart TV, which means it can access the Internet through Wi-Fi (wireless networking). My kids watch YouTube videos on it more often than they watch actual television programming. YouTube claims one billion (that's with a "b") unique monthly users who watch six billion (again with a "b") hours of video every month as of March 2013.[8] That number doubled from only three billion hours in August 2012.

✪ YouTube reaches more U.S. adults between the ages of 18 and 34 than any cable network.[9]

Let's not leave out the new kid on the block, Google Plus. In less than two years, G+ rocketed to become the second largest social media site in the world.[10] In my opinion, G+ is so relevant and well-connected to Google's other products and services that it could become the most frequented social media property within the next five years. It has quickly surged beyond my beloved Twitter to the top of the list of my most-used social networking sites.

⭐ It's not uncommon to see Google Plus abbreviated to G+ or Google+. All of these spellings are commonly accepted references to Google's social media platform.

Now let's throw mobile devices (smartphones, tablet computers) into the mix. Remember, GWI cited mobile as a catalyst for the growth surge of social media in 2013. The Internet and social media changed how we do things on a daily basis. On the heels of that shift, a new way to gather information and share it broadsided us: mobile technology. Yes, wireless mobile phones existed as early as 1973 and hit retail stores by 1983, but not everyone wanted to carry a brick-sized device around to make a call.[11] (Remember the monster cell phone Gordon Gecko [Michael Douglas] used in *Wall Street?*)

While you and I went about our business as usual, largely unconcerned about the Gordon Geckos of the world wheeling and dealing, engineers in technology kept looking for ways to make wireless mobile phones practical. As technology improved, developers in the 1990s gave us the ability to transfer data over mobile devices. It was a slow and laborious process, so again, not widely popular. (Think dial-up Internet modems.)

Then came the invention of something called 3G broadband, a technology that allowed even greater speeds of wireless data transfer. The advent of 3G changed the design of mobile phones. Devices became more compact and easier to slip into your pocket or purse. By 2007 there were 295 million subscribers on 3G networks worldwide, which was only 9 percent of the total mobile phone subscriber base.[12]

Boy, did the concept take off! Today there are over 2.1 billion subscribers to 3G and 4G (even faster) networks. You may find it surprising to know that 25 percent of U.S. consumers of the mobile Web (those who access the Internet on their mobile devices) are mobile-only users.[13] That means a quarter of U.S. mobile device users who access the Internet do so *only* on their mobile device, rarely or never on a desktop or laptop computer.

✪ Twenty-five percent of U.S. consumers of the mobile Web (those who access the Internet on their mobile devices) are mobile-only users.[14]

We use technology to connect us to information and we use it to remain in contact with people and businesses we find interesting. Mobile has become our new hobby, our new method to stay informed, and our new recreation.[15]

- ◆ 29% of you say your mobile phone is the first thing you look at each day
- ◆ 66% of you take your mobile device with you during your lunch break
- ◆ 46% of you browse the Internet with your mobile phone at least twice a week
- ◆ 61% of you use your mobile device while you watch television
- ◆ 68% of you place your mobile phone next to your bed every night

Okay, enough with the statistics already; even I'm tired of them.

What does all this mean for you? We look to the Internet, through our computers and more recently via mobile devices, for the businesses, goods, and services we need daily.[16] When a mobile user spends 84 percent of their time online looking at maps, it's frequently because they're looking to find something they need at that exact moment.[17]

The fastest growing demographic on social media sites is people over the age of 45; they're the consumers with money to spend. If those consumers can't find your business online when they're looking at a map or popular social media site, you don't exist.

That was the bad news. Let's get to some good news. If you can embrace the fact that the way we communicate has changed, then there's hope for you. This book will teach you how, when, and where to navigate through social media to grow your existing business or start the business you've always dreamed of owning.

A New Approach to Marketing Your Business

There are many ways to market your business. The Internet and social media are not the be-all and end-all of your marketing plan. Social media is an ever-growing component that needs to be carefully crafted and included in that plan. Relying on the Yellow Pages, Valpak, and face-to-face networking is no longer enough. Quite frankly, at least one of those three is a complete waste of money and time in my opinion, and it rhymes with Fellow Wages.

(⊗) Relying on the Yellow Pages, Valpak, and face-to-face networking is no longer enough. Online yellow pages directories received 5 billion searches combined in 2012. While that sounds like a healthy trend, it pales in comparison to the 6 billion Google searches *per day* during the same period of time.[18]

We boomers need a new approach to social media that makes sense based on how we learned to communicate. The boomers who have it figured out have pulled out of the driveway and are cruising the highway, enjoying the sights. They're following a strategy, not throwing spaghetti at the wall and seeing what sticks. That's not a strategy, it's desperation. Desperation quickly leads to burn-out. If you burn out and give up, you'll never reap the reward that social media and digital marketing can bring to your business.

How did I get so smart? Remember when I mentioned that I couldn't stand the idea of getting on Facebook? It seemed like such a colossal waste of time. My first post, on March 24, 2009, was "Here she is everybody!" as if the entire world was waiting for my arrival. I wasn't feeling too enthusiastic about the whole thing. Like you, I knew that it was important for my business – and if it was important, then I'd better figure it out.

In the beginning my Facebook posts were about my family or me. I joined in on real-time Twitter conversations about current events, news, and entertainment. The conversations quickly became addictive and a huge time-suck, so much so that I got disgusted and quit, cold turkey, for several months. I couldn't handle the time drain that social media caused and get the stuff done that I should be doing in my business.

It wasn't until 2010 that I began to see that a good way to get traction was to interact with the people I had met in person at various conferences and events. That meant one-on-one conversations online. Rather than push my ideas and marketing out to the world via social media, my Internet efforts consisted of interacting with people I had already met in real life. It was a different kind of networking and a different way of communicating with my network.

It takes a mind shift to embrace social media and understand the value it can add to your business. Once you embrace the shift and absorb it into your way of thinking and being, everything changes.

What You Need to Know

♦ People 45-54 years old (the young boomers and their younger siblings) make up the fastest growth in users on both Facebook (46 percent growth) and Google Plus (56 percent).

♦ YouTube visitors watch over six billions hours of video every month.

♦ Twenty-five percent of U.S. consumers of the mobile Web (those who access the Internet on their mobile devices) are mobile-only users.

♦ The fastest growing demographic on all social networking sites is people over the age of 45.

* * * * * *

CHAPTER TWO

BEST OF

How Smart Businesses Are Succeeding

Strive not to be a success, but rather to be of value.

~ ALBERT EINSTEIN

I F YOU'RE GOING to have a presence online, social media must be a huge part of your digital world. Having a website is important. Every business should own real estate, and a website is one of the simplest ways to do that. Yet there are businesses without websites that drive traffic using social media and generate tremendous leads and income.

⭐ During a recent interview for my podcast *ACT LOCAL Marketing for Small Business,* author and marketing strategist David Newman shared a statistic that shocked me. While doing research for his recent book, *Do It! Marketing: 77 Instant-Action Ideas to Boost Sales, Maximize Profits and Crush Your Competition,* he ran across a recent study that said 38 percent of U.S. small businesses still do not have a website.[1]

Social media doesn't have to be difficult or time consuming to work. Let's look at examples of businesses that sell directly to the consumer.

Tourist-Destination Gift Store on a Shoestring Budget

Feather Your Nest was a B2C specialty store located in Eureka Springs, Arkansas (a historic tourist destination in the Ozarks). The store sold homemade and vintage-looking gifts direct to consumers. Owner Gina Drennon created and successfully ran Feather Your Nest from 2003 to 2011. A web developer since the late 1990s, Drennon began using social media for the store by creating both Facebook and Twitter pages to highlight her existing website and blog.

"Eureka Springs is a tourist resort with literally dozens and dozens of shops. We stand out in the crowd because very few [of those shops] are active in social media. Very few

businesses here sell online, and those that do have not seen the success that we have." Eureka Springs is old world, midwestern, mountain country that's not on the forefront of technology changes. Not even use of the Internet had begun to blossom among small business owners. In that type of environment, an entrepreneur like Drennon could position her store to pull ahead, and she did.[2]

On a shoestring budget Drennon managed to position her store and differentiate it because her competition ignored the opportunity. Now you're asking, "If Eureka Springs isn't an Internet-savvy place, why would using social media make a difference for Feather Your Nest?" and that is a great question. The answer lies in the underlying purpose of the Internet and social media: communication.

Drennon experienced remarkable success using social media. "I've seen our web stats increase, followers increase, interactions increase, and most importantly, sales increase. But not only that, I've made many meaningful connections, with bloggers and magazine editors who have featured our products and our store, that bring us huge amounts of attention that you really cannot put a price on. I can positively say that at *least half* of the national press we've received is due to contacts we've made over social media."

Although the number of fans and followers that the company attracted was relatively small, the amount of interaction on Feather Your Nest's Facebook and Twitter pages created big results in their local marketplace.

Organic Ice Cream Maker Goes Beyond Local

Luna and Larry's Coconut Bliss, an Oregon-based organic ice cream maker, is another great case study of a small business that uses social media to position its products in the local market.[3] The company's use of social media helped it to grow beyond local. Owners Luna Marcus and Larry Kaplowitz tell their story of humble beginnings in 2004. They purchased a hand-cranked ice cream machine from Goodwill for $1.50 and began experimenting with a base of organic coconut milk and natural agave sweetener.

For months Luna and Larry held tasting parties in their home. Their friends and neighbors could try new flavors, give feedback, and go home with a hand-packed pint or two of

Coconut Bliss. Two local shop owners who attended a tasting asked the pair to start making Coconut Bliss for their local specialty stores, and the rest is history. Now Luna and Larry's Coconut Bliss comes in a variety of flavors and is available in most natural food stores in the United States and Canada. What started as a B2C enterprise expanded into a B2B company. Social media was a driver for both.

What did Luna and Larry do right? Let's have a looksee.

They make a habit of using fun and friendly images of real customers enjoying their product. They use those same images on their website and across all social media platforms. They began with Facebook and Twitter, where they shared not just images but other content that appeals to people who buy and consume all-natural, vegetarian products. It's common to find vegan recipes, photos from local Farmer's Markets, and shout-outs to other companies engaged in social goodness on the Coconut Bliss Facebook and Twitter streams.

This strategy gained Coconut Bliss visibility among its ideal target market and created joint partnerships with people and companies that share its values. The company makes a habit of engaging with customers and brand advocates. It even goes so far as to champion the causes of its customers by sharing user-submitted photos and videos from live events on the company social media newsfeeds.

Luna and Larry were smart not to stop with Facebook and Twitter. You can find them on Google Plus and YouTube as well, which is important for more reasons than just building a social following.

As a local business, Coconut Bliss's Google+ profile helps it appear in results of local Google searches. The company's YouTube account (called a channel) contains simple videos describing its products in a likable and relatable way that helps you get to know the owners. The extra benefit is that the videos show up in search results too.

In short, Luna and Larry's Coconut Bliss uses social media to celebrate followers and share their stories. The result is a loyal fan base that stays connected and engaged, causing a ripple effect that draws new fans to the brand.

Wife, Mother, Homemaker, and Carpenter Empowers Women

This next example is interesting and I think you'll enjoy it. Meet Ana White, homemaker.[4] Ana is a wife and mother and, yes, a "homemaker." A carpenter, Ana, along with her husband, built their Alaska home from the ground up. Ana designs and builds furniture. Since 2009 she has been publishing free how-to guides empowering other women to do the same.

Using good social media strategy, Ana engages with fans daily on her Facebook page (with over 250,000 likes). She publishes a "Brag Post of the Day," where she shares fan photos of projects completed from her how-to plans.  This puts the spotlight on her followers and highlights their accomplishments. People love to talk about themselves, so this approach is a win!

In addition to Facebook, Ana White makes excellent use of Pinterest. Pinterest is an image-heavy social media site, so photos of do-it-yourself projects are a natural fit. She publishes project tutorials for every room in your house, offering inspiration and guidance that her nearly 60,000 followers love. Pinterest is popular among women, so the medium and the user base fit exactly into White's marketing plan.

On YouTube, White has over 13,000 subscribers to her channel. She posts videos on everything from how to build and attach kitchen cabinets to how to build a doll bed with your daughter. Her success on social media gave her the platform to write a book called *The Handbuilt Home: 34 Simple, Stylish, and Budget-Friendly Woodworking Projects for Every Room*. The book was a #1 Amazon Best Seller in the Furniture & Carpentry section. All this exposure has made her website attractive to sponsors, who pay to advertise on her site.

Local Restaurant Opening Is Grand

My final B2C example is of a local restaurant in my community, which was also a client of mine at the time. This restaurant was building its flagship location and planning the grand opening from May through July of 2012. The owners were smart enough to know they could not just throw their

doors open in August and expect a stampede of interested foodies. They needed to create some buzz to get patrons interested. That's where I stepped in.

We crafted a marketing campaign for the restaurant using flyers that employees handed out all over town at the weekly farmer's market and networking events. The flyer included details of the restaurant such as its logo, name, address and phone number, style of food, and what appeared to be a yellow Post-It note that said, "Text

'word' to ##### to be on our VIP list at the Grand Opening!"
The 'word' was a part of the restaurant's name and the #####
was our particular texting short code.

⊗ To set up a texting program like this, you first need
to buy service from a text message service provider.
Choosing the right provider is important. First, check
that you can buy a word from the provider that works
for your business before you use it in print or any
other type of advertising. It can be difficult to get a
generic, popular word such as burger, for example.
Consider using part of the business name or a service
feature, which will likely be easier to get. First buy the
word, test it, then print it.

☛ The texting short code is a five- or six-digit number
that customers will send their text to, such as 252525,
for example. The texting service will give you the
short code, and it varies by provider. The codes are
typically simple and repetitive.

When leads opted in to our text messaging campaign
they received automatic text responses updating them on the
construction and ever-drifting opening date. We asked for
their email addresses so we could encourage them to follow
the restaurant on Facebook and Twitter. We also posted photos of the construction process, menu updates, and generally
kept prospective patrons informed of our progress.

The result was a list of over 300 highly engaged customers who were anticipating the opening of this restaurant.
They filled it to bursting, with a line out the door of people
waiting to get in on opening night (which was a Monday –

typically the slowest night for a restaurant) and for several nights afterward. The text-messaging campaign was an ideal way to avoid the "if you build it, they will come" mistake that many small businesses make.

Marketing with social media is a no-brainer for the business-to-consumer company, but it's often more difficult to envision how to use social media if your company is strictly business-to-business oriented. Here are two purely B2B examples of using social media to increase business.

Electronic Marketplace Supports the Marine Industry

ShipServ helps marine and offshore buyers to find suppliers, trade efficiently, and build trusted relationships. The company has over 8,000 ships and rigs, 200 ship owners/managers, and over 45,000 suppliers in its network.

In 2008 ShipServ came to the realization that its image in the marine community was as nothing more than a software company. Its customers were not early adopters of technology, and making a shift to an online service from traditional purchasing channels was a big hurdle. In spite of this chal-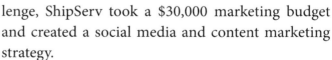lenge, ShipServ took a $30,000 marketing budget and created a social media and content marketing strategy.

The strategy started with an overhaul of its website, including search engine optimization. It launched a blog, created and published a series of free reports, and opened a LinkedIn group for its community. Three months into the effort, ShipServ broke even on its investment. The number of website visitors increased by 59 percent, and social media traffic (from LinkedIn and Twitter) went from zero to being one of the company's top 20 sources of leads.[5] The lack of online community translated into an opportunity. As technology adoption continued to rise in its market, ShipServ was perfectly positioned to take advantage. The company created an opportunity to become the go-to resource by having social media outlets already in place, which they've done quite successfully.

Solder Can Be Exciting

The second B2B example is Indium Corporation, a global manufacturer and supplier of solder and related materials to the electronics assembly industry. Sexy, right? How and why would they make use of social media? Indium used it to demonstrate thought leadership, build relationships, generate leads, and drive sales.

Indium enlisted its engineers to blog about soldering, flux cleaning, and tombstoning. Don't ask me what all that stuff is because I don't know, but that's not the point. These are topics that Indium engineers are experts on and could easily and comfortably write about in their own voices, showing and sharing their personalities. They wrote blog posts on Facebook and Twitter, and they expanded their outreach by creating YouTube demonstration videos.

The company achieved several results. Indium was able to show that it's unique in its industry. Sharing its employees' knowledge firmly defined them as industry leaders. Industry trade magazine editors noticed the blog posts through social sharing. Subsequently those editors invited employees to contribute articles. Indium was also invited to events and conferences, where employees presented technical papers, which reinforced their standing as thought leaders and further enhanced the company's brand.[6]

In the final analysis, B2B decision makers are people who go online to research before making a buying decision, just as they do in their personal decision making. According to Forrester Research, two-thirds to 90 percent of the buying cycle (the steps prospective customers go through before they buy) is complete before a B2B buyer ever speaks with a sales rep. This is because the online world gives buyers the opportunity to research and engage with businesses directly. It's not in your firm's best interest to ignore social media or view it as a limited tool. The Internet is a tool for communication, and when you use it *right,* good things happen.

What You Need to Know

♦ Both B2B (business-to-business) and B2C (business-to-consumer) companies use social media to drive business.

♦ The most successful local businesses connect online marketing with offline marketing strategies and activities to reach more prospects.

♦ Successful businesses create opportunities for free media exposure and public relations through the thoughtful use of social media.

♦ Social media is an easy way to stay top-of-mind with your prospects.

Note: Appendix A shows you how to sign up for Facebook, Twitter, LinkedIn, Pinterest, Google Plus, and YouTube accounts and how to set up your business profile on each of these social media destinations.

CHAPTER THREE

✦ ✦ ✦ ✦ ✦

BEFORE YOU LEAVE

Navigating the Digital Highway

I see my path, but I don't know where it leads. Not knowing where I'm going is what inspires me to travel it.

~ ROSALIA DE CASTRO

ETTING SOCIAL MEDIA MARKETING RIGHT is both simple and complex. As with many problems you face, the solution is not rocket science. Each of the individual parts of your social media strategy is simple to create when you know what you're doing. Adding all the simple little pieces together creates a more complex whole. When looked at from the outside, that whole seems much more difficult than it truly is. Do you view the Internet and social media as tools for marketing? Does the idea of using social media for marketing leave you confused, feeling like an outsider looking in?

This travel guide is going to bring you inside the digital world. It includes step-by-step, simple instructions that are going to help you understand the world of social media marketing. Then you can build a Marketing Action Plan (MAP) that's just right for your business. Working through this book should feel like planning a trip. You can decide where you want to visit, how you're going to get there, what to do while you're there, and in the end you'll have established a road map that's unique for you and your business. Let me give you some more details so you can see where we're heading.

What the Trip Will Look Like

A trip always starts with, "Where do you want to go?" We'll start our plan by looking in depth at the six most important social media destinations for baby boomer business owners. Depending on your business, some destinations may not be interesting to you. But you do need to know what and where they are, and the types of people who frequent them, so you can make an informed decision whether to visit a particular destination. Once you've chosen one of my three suggested itineraries, I'll share more on the language, etiquette, and transportation alternatives open to you as well as insider tips to get you started.

You'll discover five steps for learning to speak the language in this new digital world you'll visit. You also need to know the four secrets to blending in like a native and the three best methods for arriving at and traveling within each social media site on your itinerary. There are two roads you can travel to reach each destination, so we'll discuss each one and why you may want to choose one over the other.

The end result of this process is one roadmap that will guide your travel to any or all of the six destinations covered in this guide. You'll become a safe, successful, and savvy social media traveler, building your business without wasting time.

I've mentioned that there are only six destinations I want you to consider visiting. Are there more social media sites on the planet? Of course! But only six are going to be worth your time and effort as you get started. When you're a more seasoned traveler, you decide to visit smaller, unique destinations. But remember that these sites won't serve you in the beginning the same way that the first six can when it comes to marketing your business.

What are the six websites? Clearly you skipped the introduction! You've likely heard of them all, and there's a reason for that. They're the most popular and highly visited social networking sites on the Internet. We'll explore Facebook, Twitter, LinkedIn, Pinterest, Google Plus, and YouTube. Yes, YouTube is a social media site; in fact it's one of the top three most trafficked websites on the Internet.

As I mentioned earlier, there are five steps you need to take to learn the language of social media. The language of social media is really about content. What exactly are you going to talk about when you visit? What should you leave behind after you've made initial contact with people and businesses so potential leads will remember you? It's important that you're able to answer these questions and apply what you learn, otherwise you'll end up spinning your wheels. These five steps are: Keep It Simple Stupid, Keep It Social, Tell a Story, Make It Scalable, and Have a Strategy. Becoming well versed in each step will help you build relationships with your ideal prospects.

CHECKLIST
- ✓ Destination
- ✓ Language
- ✓ Etiquette
- ✓ Transport
- ✓ Timing

Once you understand the language of social media, you're poised for success. You will already know more than 99 percent of business owners who attempt to use social media for marketing. The road gets much easier from here as we move on to the four features of your content. Once mastered, these features will help you blend in like a native at any social media website you travel to. How you engage potential customers will determine whether they come back for more. How you say the message is as important as the message itself in social media. We'll tackle the concepts of accessibility, transparency, consistency, and influence in the content you share with other visitors. Understanding these concepts is an important step toward building a thriving community that looks forward to hearing what only you can share.

Now we're really moving and this engine is building steam. At this point you will have learned how to pack for your trip – what content you're going to bring with you to share – and you understand the various languages of social media. Your next decision will be to decide which modes of transportation you're going to use to deliver your content. Believe it or not, there are only three ways to share your message in the digital world. I'm going to describe all three and give you insider secrets to streamline your efforts. The choices are simple. You will either hand deliver all your content personally, automate its delivery, or some combination of the two. Remember, I said it ain't rocket science!

At this point in developing your MAP you will have chosen a specific itinerary to explore that makes sense for developing your business. You'll know the steps for creating great content to share at those destinations and how you intend to deliver that content. The bulk of the work will be done. The next step in your plan will be to choose one of two roads to travel to reach all the important sights along your journey.

The itinerary you choose will have an impact on which roads you travel. You can move from one road to the other as you like, but eventually you'll find that you prefer one to the other. You have to decide how you want to manage your time. You have two choices: do-it-yourself or have someone do it for you. No matter which road you choose, it's important for you to have a deep understanding of your MAP, especially if you're the driver. Even if you decide to outsource the implementation of your marketing action plan, you still want to be able to lead the tour.

Finishing Touches

That's it! The end result is that you've planned a journey to engage in social media to grow your business. As your faithful guide, I will be here to help you put the finishing touches on your MAP. This MAP will become your one strategy for using social media to grow your business.

Social media doesn't have to be time consuming to work, but the options are overwhelming. Should you be pinning or posting or plus'ing? Like any new-fangled thing-a-ma-bob, once you understand it, using it becomes easy peasy. Suddenly you can't imagine your life, or in this case your business, running without it.

⊗ Taking a scattershot approach to marketing wastes time and resources. It's faster in the beginning but wastes time in the end. Careful planning upfront will ensure that you enjoy your travels through the digital world. A little effort now will make your life easier down the road.

Once you know where people are and why they congregate at any given social networking site, you'll begin to see the opportunities. Sharing your goods and services with people who are ideal prospects gets so much easier. Knowing the language and how to "talk" to folks on any social media site will give you confidence to get behind the wheel and travel to places unknown. You're bound to discover a new favorite hideaway where people are looking for exactly what only you can deliver.

What You Need to Know

♦ Your strategy will center around six social media sites: Facebook, Twitter, LinkedIn, Pinterest, Google Plus, and YouTube.

♦ There are five simple steps to creating content that your ideal prospects and customers want.

♦ Packing efficiently is a skill. In social media terms, how you bring messages to each site involves some time management and simple technology knowledge.

♦ There is some groundwork that has to happen before you make use of any social media site for business. This groundwork is important and will make your trip to each social media destination more successful.

CHAPTER FOUR

✦ ✦ ✦ ✦ ✦

ITINERARIES
The Most Important Social Media Destinations

You have brains in your head. You have feet in your shoes. You can steer yourself any direction you choose. You're on your own. And you know what you know. And YOU are the one who'll decide where to go . . .

~ DR. SEUSS

HALF THE BATTLE of using social media to build your business lies in knowing where to show up. That's why I've narrowed down the landscape to the six destinations you should concern yourself with as you plan your journey. Are there more places to go? Without a doubt! Should you visit them all? That depends on how adventurous you are. As you get to know your way around the six social networking sites I recommend, it might benefit you to venture beyond the six, so I recommend you visit other sites to check them out.

One of my goals is to help you use social media effectively. To do that requires keeping you on track. It's easy to get

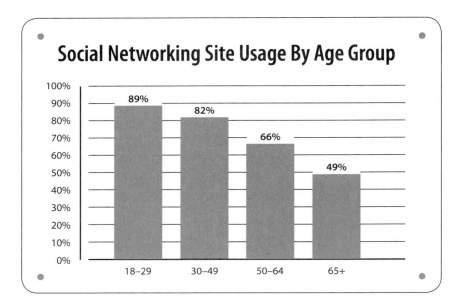

The graphic above shows a breakdown of social networking site usage by age group in the United States as of January 2014.[1] As you would imagine, younger users are the largest consumers of social media. But the number of boomers (50–64) and 65+ users may surprise you.

distracted online, and it's likely that you will. Entrepreneurs call it the "shiny object syndrome." It's easy to get distracted by the next "up and coming," "everybody says I should be using it" thing online, and this is especially true in social media circles. Remember, we have a specific goal in mind – to learn how to use social media to grow your business.

You can see in Social Media's Top 10 Highlights in the "Introduction" that there are more than six social networking sites that could be valuable to your marketing strategy. Certain sites resonate more than others with particular age groups. We're going to begin planning our trip to locations where consumers over the age of 30 tend to spend time and money.

Again, the six destinations we will examine are Facebook, Twitter, LinkedIn, Pinterest, Google Plus, and YouTube. Let's start by asking the same questions you would ask before taking any trip: Where is it? What is there to do? Who else will be there?

Three Itineraries to Choose From

To prepare well and not waste any time, let's narrow down your choices even further. I want to start by identifying which social media targets make the most sense for your particular business. Then you can choose the itinerary that best meets your needs. The six travel destinations fall into three market categories: B2C, B2B, or both. I suggest you choose the one that most closely fits your business, and plan to add the second and even third, as part of your MAP down the road. The three most popular itineraries in social media travel are On The Street, Enterprise, and Crossroads.

The On The Street tour is for B2C businesses, those companies that are primarily business-to-consumer oriented. B2C includes storefronts, retail establishments, restaurants, and service providers such as insurance agents, health practitioners, and real estate agents who deal with individual consumers. On The Street is an engaging and friendly tour where travelers speak about not only business but about any number of subjects that naturally occur in the B2C world. It's the Internet version of the general store, a place where people purchase the goods they need and

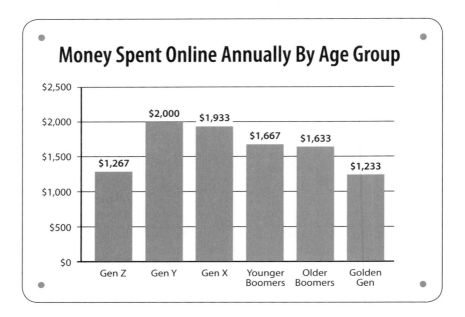

Money Spent Online Annually By Age Group

The graph shows values: Gen Z $1,267; Gen Y $2,000; Gen X $1,933; Younger Boomers $1,667; Older Boomers $1,633; Golden Gen $1,233. Y-axis: $0 to $2,500.

★ The graphic above shows that not only do Americans look online to research before they buy but they spend money online, too. Boomers (combining younger and older boomers) spend 50% more than the next highest age group.[2]

where they gather to build relationships with other members of the community.

The Enterprise tour is ideal for B2B businesses, which provide goods and services primarily to other businesses rather than directly to the consumer. If you're responsible for business development and need to speak with company decision makers, this is the tour for you. You'll visit the places where decision makers are more likely to be engaging. The atmosphere is generally professional, with just enough personality shared to build the rapport that leads to conversation.

The Crossroads tour is for businesses that serve both B2C and B2B markets. Crossroads can stand alone, but it's also the best add-on itinerary after planning your On The Street or Enterprise trip.

B2B BUSINESS
Take the Enterprise Tour

Our six social media destinations fall into these three itineraries nicely. If your business is B2C category, you should plan an On The Street tour, which takes you to Facebook and Pinterest as the most important destinations to market your business. If your business is B2B, you should plan an Enterprise tour where Twitter and LinkedIn are the best places to begin your social media marketing. The intersection of B2C and B2B business is where a Crossroads tour of Google Plus and YouTube thrives. You should tour these social

BOTH B2C & B2B
Take the Crossroads Tour

media destinations regardless of what market category you initially see your business aligning with, or if your customers actually straddle both markets.

Next, you need to understand the culture of each social media destination to determine where your ideal prospects are. Let's take a look at the history and highlights of each so you can discover the best of social media.

Destination: Facebook
What Is It and Who Uses It?

Facebook was founded in 2004 by Mark Zuckerberg, who was a college student at the time. The film *The Social Network* immortalized the origins of Facebook, but it has grown up quite a bit since its humble beginnings in a college setting. It's still the number one social media website with 1.32 billion estimated monthly active users worldwide.[3] It's typically the number-two-ranked website visited on the Internet after Google. You can find the site at www.facebook.com.

Both men and women in the United States use Facebook, with women using it just a tad bit more often (53 percent of users are women). According to a 2013 Pew Research study, 71 percent of all U.S. adult Internet users visit Facebook.[4] The demographics on Facebook continue to grow yearly. In the United States, of people 18–29 years old who use the Internet, 86 percent use Facebook. The same study found that 56 percent of those 30–49 years old use Facebook, and nearly 43 percent of those 50–64 years old are users. There are even Facebook user statistics for the 65-and-over crowd, which includes my own mother, by the way. A noteworthy 32 percent of those 65 and older use Facebook.

Facebook is the most popular social media app (software) on smartphones, and it accounts for 66 percent of total social media sharing on iPhones alone. While Facebook data still skews young, as will be the case with most social media sites, the group of users 45–54 years old has seen a 45 percent growth since year-end 2012. You may also want to note that 75 percent of U.S. college-educated people use Facebook. There's significant buying power in those numbers. It explains why brands use Facebook to reach potential customers – a large number of their prospects visit Facebook daily.

As of June 2014 Facebook had 1.07 billion monthly active users through mobile devices. They had 829 million daily active users on average, with around 150 million of them being in the United States and Canada.

With all these people visiting Facebook daily, you're probably wondering what they do there. Facebook has a variety of things to see and do. Every active user of the site has a personal profile, where they can show personal details such as where they are in the world, who their friends and family members are, where they went to school, where they work, what movies, books, and television they enjoy . . . and the list goes on. A personal profile on Facebook can share any information that you would share with friends in a social setting – it's a snapshot of your life.

Businesses have profiles on Facebook, too, called business pages. People interact with business pages in much the same way they do with other people. A business page is akin to putting a face and personality on a company.

Another feature of Facebook is Groups. People or businesses form groups where like-minded individuals can interact. Groups can be public or private. An example of a group would be a high school graduating class or college alumni. Both are likely to be private groups, open only to the individuals who graduated in a certain year or attended a particular university. A public group could be the attendees from a conference who want to stay in touch and continue to network.

Both people and businesses post articles, images, videos, and written updates to their profiles and in groups. Friends and followers can see these updates, images, and videos. These friends and followers comment on your content and Facebook notifies you of the activity. Then you can return and reply to comments. This is how conversations happen. Another form of interaction is the "Like" button which is Facebook jargon for the proverbial "thumbs up." When your followers really enjoy your content, they can even share it directly to their own news feed, which expands your reach to their network of friends.

Facebook is a good social media site to start with, especially if you own a B2C business. That's why you'll see big brands such as Walmart, Amazon, Nike, Coca-Cola, and Starbucks using Facebook to such a large degree. Consumers enjoy engaging with brands on Facebook and interacting with a more human side of the business. Even B2B companies are using Facebook to boost their engagement levels with other businesses. Building relationships in the informal atmosphere of Facebook works in the business-to-business marketplace as well.

In fact, a 2012 study conducted by IBM of 1,709 CEOs in 64 countries found that over the next three to five years, those leaders anticipate that their companies will scale back on traditional media by 61 percent and increase their social media presence by 256 percent. This is happening for one simple reason – because social media is where the potential customers are.[5]

There's a great website for Chief Marketing Officers called CMO.com that publishes an infographic each year called The CMOs Guide to the Social Landscape.[6] They rank current social networking sites on a scale of Good, OK, or Bad for customer communication, brand awareness, traffic to your website, and SEO (search engine optimization). In 2014 CMO.com rated Facebook as Good for all categories except brand awareness, which they rated as OK, stating, "Facebook allows for easy posting of links, photos, and videos. Yet a recent survey of 100-plus brand pages shows organic reach fell 49 percent in the four months after October 2013." That's a decline from 2012 and 2013 rankings in which CMO.com had ranked Facebook as Good in the brand awareness category. The opposite occurred relative to Facebook and SEO. In the 2012 and 2013 reports, CMO.com ranked Facebook as

OK for search engine optimization, but in 2014 the site received a Good ranking. This occurred because Google made changes in their criteria for ranking web pages in search results. "Facebook shares, comments, and likes are among the top social media activities determining how high a web page gets ranked in Google search results . . ."

Remember, the whole point of social media is communication. Facebook is a winner from that standpoint, whether you directly engage the consumer or other businesses. Everybody seems to be there.

Destination: Twitter
What Is It and Who Uses It?

Twitter is a particular favorite of mine. It's the favorite of Fortune 500 companies, too. In fact, it's become so important to the social networking landscape that we invented a new word just to describe it – *microblog*. No matter what label we slap on it, Twitter is a communication tool and you can find it at www.twitter.com.

Invented in 2006 by the Odeo company, Twitter was born out of SMS (short message service) technology, or text messaging. In 2007 Twitter was spun off as a separate company. Twitter lets you send text-based messages called tweets, which are limited to 140 characters. This limit makes Twitter both challenging and the most rapidly paced social networking platform out there.

★ Short Message Service (SMS) is the technology that gives us the ability to send text-only messages on a mobile device and is limited to 160 characters in length. Multimedia Messaging Service (MMS) is the standard way to send multimedia content, such as video or images, to and from mobile devices. The technology is built into your smartphone.

It can be a bit like watching a stock ticker if you don't know the ins and outs of organizing Twitter to make it useful for your business. On Twitter you can follow as many other users as you like without their permission, and, likewise, users can follow you without your okay. It's a very open platform in that regard. You can also block users whom you find objectionable from following your account. It doesn't take much time to end up following and being followed by thousands of users, and all those messages fly by on your stream.

With over 500 million tweets (what we call content messages on Twitter) sent per day and 271 million active users talking almost simultaneously, Twitter is full of noise. From a demographic view, the older you are, the less likely you are to use Twitter. If you're a city dweller you're significantly more likely to be using social media in general – and Twitter specifically. People 55–64 years old are the fastest growing demographic on Twitter, increasing 79 percent from 2012 to 2013, and the female-to-male ratio here is 50/50.[7]

Twitter is one of the more complicated social networking platforms because it has many more "rules" you need to know to use it correctly. There's also a vocabulary and culture that has evolved around Twitter, including this biggie – the *hashtag*. A hashtag is created by using the pound sign in front of a word, such as #Boomer. Hashtags make it easier for users to find information on specific topics (like Boomers). We used to call this symbol the pound sign or number sign, but because of Twitter it's almost universally referred to as a hashtag now. In fact, hashtags on Twitter have become so prevalent that Facebook began using them, as do Google Plus and Instagram. They're part of our social communication vernacular. We use hashtags to organize conversation and gain more control in navigating what would otherwise be an unruly landscape.

Unlike Facebook, where you can speak in full sentences and paragraphs, on Twitter you must get your message out economically. You'll see abbreviations, letters missing in words, or single letters used in place of words to fit the message into the limited space allowed – tweets such as "Great deals 4 u today @Store21! Stop by & use code TWTR 2 get an xtra discount!"

Twitter is unique because of its limitations. Having a 140-character limit to each message is quite challenging, so users often speak in headlines and share links to articles that their audiences might find interesting. They may also speak in "sales talk" and offer deals or use coupon-type language, as in the example above, to leverage the reach of Twitter while still getting their message out. Rather than conversational, tweets are short and usually informational. You may have heard that Twitter is where people tell each other what they had for breakfast and where they are at the moment. While I'm sure those tweets happen every day, they are an infinitesimal part of the types of messages you will encounter.

★ This sentence is 140 characters, the maximum length of a tweet – more than you might think, but keeping to 140 characters requires effort.

There are several ways to converse on Twitter besides tweeting your own content messages. You can share the online web address of an article you know your followers would enjoy. A quicker interaction is to click the star icon, which is the Twitter version of "thumbs up" or "Like," or you can retweet. A retweet is taking another user's tweet and sharing it on your stream. When a user retweets your content, they are exposing you to all of their followers, promoting growth of your account.

There are dozens of third-party websites to make Twitter easier for the active user. For example, a common activity on Twitter is chats. Here's one instance where hashtags come into play. During a chat session on Twitter, everyone who wants to take part in the conversation follows the same hashtag, such as #BizHeroes for example. The host interviews the guest while participants follow along and have a conversation about the topic. A great site for participating in Twitter chats is Tweetchat.com. This is a third-party website designed solely for participating in a Twitter chat, making it easy to focus and engage in that one activity among the thousands that are flying by on your general Twitter stream.

Twitter is also used by many brands to deal with customer service issues. The best customer service departments in big organizations have an eye on Twitter and watch for complaints. Often users will post messages and use the company's Twitter handle, such as @Store21 in the example above, to publicly tweet their messages to the company. (The "@" sign followed by a username is used for mentioning or replying to the user. In this example Store 21 would get a copy of the tweet in which their Twitter handle was used). This is one of the better ways to get help when you're having an issue with a company's product or service.

In 2014 CMO.com rated The Social Landscape of Twitter above that of Facebook, with a level of Good across all four categories: SEO, customer communication, brand exposure, and traffic to your website. According to CMO.com, there is more opportunity on Twitter to spread your brand message in a viral way: "Excellent for branding and PR management." Like Facebook, Twitter also gets a Good rating for SEO, which is new for the Twitter platform. It seems that tweets about a Web page are gaining influence in Google search rankings and are among the top ten most important ranking factors. This means that tweeting about your business and including a link to your website is quite valuable.

Twitter is a great place to start if your business is a B2B company but isn't limited to the B2B space. Brands are popular on Twitter, as are individuals and celebrities. One of the great things about Twitter is that it's easy to find important and influential people and engage them in conversation. There are many opportunities to get publicity and forge relationships with the media, authors you like, and even CEOs of corporations. You don't have to be "friends" with people to see what they're saying on Twitter or to tweet a message to them. While it's fast moving, it's also more open. There are no gatekeepers between you and the person you want to engage with.

Destination: LinkedIn
What Is It and Who Uses It?

Chances are you already use LinkedIn because it's the primary business professional social networking website. If you don't use LinkedIn you may want to start there with your social media journey. Everyone from high school through retirement should have a profile on LinkedIn because that profile acts as your resume online. *All* Fortune 500 companies have executives as members on LinkedIn, and 88 of the Fortune 100 use its corporate recruiting membership classification, called Talent Solutions.[8] LinkedIn rounds out what most people consider the top three social media sites (Facebook and Twitter being the other two), and you can find it at www.linkedin.com.

The site was launched in May of 2003 and has over 300 million registered users, with over 100 million of those users in the United States.[9] The number of unique visitors to the site in one month rose 63 percent from June 2012 to June 2013. LinkedIn is often the first place a new networking contact will go to check you out, learn what you do, learn more about your skills and expertise, and identify how long you've been in business. They also look there to see what other people are saying about you. The site format is predefined in a way that makes it easy to determine if you're the right professional for the job, whether you're searching for employment or you're a consultant or contractor looking for B2B connections.

LinkedIn provides many opportunities to get and create business. There are job postings through companies and recruiters, and you can apply for a position directly through the site. LinkedIn also has groups where like-minded people gather, much like a Facebook group, to discuss specific topics. Remember, all activity is business-centric on LinkedIn – you will not find a vegan group sharing recipes as you might on Facebook. You will find a Vegan Professionals group and a Vegan Mainstream group, who discuss how to make their companies more vegan-friendly and share resources on how to work in non-vegan-friendly environments. You can find groups based on profession, alma maters, networking organizations, alumni of companies you may have worked for in the past, and many other categories. Within these groups you can engage with other professionals and leverage the benefit of networking on LinkedIn to build your business.

After signing up you can connect with other professionals that you already have in your Rolodex (so to speak). LinkedIn is less social than other social media sites in that you have to send a request to connect with people; potential contacts must accept your request before you gain full access to them. This is one of the many things about LinkedIn culture that makes it more professional and less cocktail-partyish. Contacts who accept your request become 1st connections. LinkedIn has a protocol that allows you to look at the Rolodex of the people who are your 1st connections. You can mine opportunities to connect with people that your 1st connections know who might be good contacts for you and your business. You can ask 1st connections for introductions to those people, get connected, and send private messages within the LinkedIn platform.

LinkedIn also lets you see 2nd and 3rd connections based on your Rolodex, which gives you additional opportunities to expand your network. You cannot speak to 2nd and 3rd connections directly, so you have to introduce yourself through a message or ask one of your 1st connections for an introduction. Always include in your request why you want to connect with that person. You will then need to wait for the introduction to be sent on your behalf and for the connection request to be accepted.

How you complete your profile on LinkedIn is extremely important – it's the first impression other professionals have of you. Your profile should include a good picture of your face to jog the memory of people you've met in person. Many LinkedIn users will not connect with someone who doesn't have a profile picture. Since you're asking them to open their Rolodex to you, it's understandable that they want to know as much about you as possible, including what you look like.

⊗ It's worth spending the time and money to have a professional headshot taken by a photographer to use as your profile picture. A common mistake made by new social media users is snapping a quick photo with a smartphone and assuming that's good enough. It isn't. First impressions matter online just as they do offline. A poor-quality photo with poor lighting as a profile picture begs the question, "What else does this person put little effort into?" That's not the kind of impression you want to make on a new connection.

There's plenty of room to share employment history, education, and organizational memberships on your profile. LinkedIn is essentially a huge professional database; the more information you share the better. There are several levels of membership available. Most professionals find the free membership is great. It allows you to have a full profile, know who has viewed your profile (in a limited capacity), see the profiles of 2nd-degree connections, and join up to 50 groups. You can even create your own group and manage it, plus you can connect with up to 30,000 people as 1st-level contacts. For most professionals this is enough. If you need more you can always upgrade your membership.

While LinkedIn is a crucial site for any business professional, from a marketing standpoint it's not as good as the other sites I've mentioned. CMO.com rated LinkedIn as Good for customer communication and brand exposure, especially personal branding, but just OK for SEO and traffic generation. LinkedIn is not the social media site you'll use to drive traffic or grow your website, but it is critical for establishing your professional credentials.

Destination: Pinterest
What Is It and Who Uses It?

A year or two ago, when I would mention Pinterest during a speaking engagement, the faces in the audience went blank. Now? Not so much. Pinterest launched in March 2010 and by 2012 boasted engagement from 21 percent of all U.S. Internet users versus 18 percent by Twitter during that same time. The people who use it love it, which is how it became the first stand-alone website in history to reach 10 million unique monthly visitors in under two years. Pinterest now drives more Internet traffic to websites than Twitter and Reddit combined. While the statistics constantly change, researchers agree that Pinterest users are overwhelmingly women, and approximately half of them have children. It's a goldmine for business brands. You can find it at www.pinterest.com.

Pinterest is a virtual corkboard and simulates scrapbooking. Every user who opens an account creates an unlimited number of boards that they can title. They then "pin" images from the web, or images that they upload from their computer or smartphone, to each board. It's primarily a visual platform based on pictures, and it's a retailer's dream. Even if you don't have a B2C retail business, you can use Pinterest to drive traffic to your other social media sites.

The demographics of Pinterest mirror the demographics of the U.S. Internet population, within 1–2 percentage points. According to Compete.com, Pinterest users aged 35–44 make up 22 percent of its users, those 45–54 make up 19 percent, those 55–64 make up 15 percent, and those over 65 make up 10 percent. Pinterest users aged 35 and over comprise 66 percent of the total user base, and they spend about 90 minutes per month on the site.

Business Insider estimated that Pinterest is worth $2.5 billion based on the fact that its 45 million active monthly users are well-educated females who like to spend their disposable income.[10] On average, a Pinterest shopper (a user who follows through to a retailer's website and makes a purchase) will spend $170 per buying visit: compare this to Facebook shoppers, who spend $95 per visit, and Twitter shoppers, who spend $70 per visit. The cost of acquiring a Pinterest user (getting the user to visit your website) is less than the cost of acquiring a Facebook user. "The current cost of acquiring a Pinterest follower is a penny to $0.50, depending on the type of business. That compares to $0.50 to $2.50 on Facebook," said Daniel Maloney, CEO of PinLeague, a consultancy that tracks social media usage.

Many brands experience great success with Pinterest by sharing images of their products – just ask retailers Nordstrom and Sephora. Popular industries that leverage Pinterest include anything design-related, such as furniture, lighting, architecture, decorating, homes, clothing, fashion, and more. Food and drink product companies also easily leverage Pinterest. In fact, 18 percent of all images shared on Pinterest are food- and drink-related. But it's not just the retail and food sectors that experience success with Pinterest; B2B and nonretail businesses can also use Pinterest. To be successful you may need to be more creative with your images. This is where the popular infographic comes into play.

People love infographics. Infographics are images that look stylish and contain statistics. You may be familiar with them – they often appear in magazines such as *Time* or *Newsweek*. Magazines use infographics as tools to illustrate timelines, complicated information that's difficult to digest, or large quantities of data. Clever graphics with pie charts, graphs, and typography that's pleasing to the eye simplify information and make it easier to understand. After all, a picture is worth a thousand words. This is a great way for B2B brands to make use of Pinterest. You can also get clever, like GE, which has over 23,000 followers with boards such as Badass Machines and Mind = Blown. It takes some ingenuity, a sense of humor, and fun to make your business or industry sector interesting.

CMO.com tells us that Pinterest is Good for brand exposure, SEO, and generating traffic to your website, but it's just OK for customer communication. The reason Pinterest gets a poorer rating for customer communication is that, until August 2014, the platform was not set up as a verbal communication tool. It was a visual medium of sharing, so users didn't have long conversations, if any. CMO.com says, "With proper technique, Pinterest can generate immense amounts of traffic to your site. Adding 'Pin It' buttons to your pages is key in getting people to share it with their friends and followers."[11]

☛ In August 2014 Pinterest added the ability to send private messages to other users. This is just one example of how social media sites are constantly evolving into better communication tools. The ability for users to speak directly to one another will help Pinterest grow and make it more valuable as a marketing tool.

Destination: Google Plus
What Is It and Who Uses It?

On June 28, 2015, Google Plus turned four years old. The youngest of all the social media sites on my list is turning into the most powerful. Google Plus, or G+, or Google+ (all correct references to the platform), was Google's fourth try at social media – and they finally got it right. Google Plus is seeing record growth, with 925,000 new users every day.[12] You can find the service at www.plus.google.com

You may discover that you already have a profile on G+. A profile requires that you have a Google email address, known as a Gmail address, which many of you already have. Some of you may have more than one, which can create some complications. For most of you, if you have a Gmail address, there's a Google Plus profile waiting for you to claim. Google may even prompt you from time to time to claim your profile, to make you aware of your opportunity to join the fun.

⊗ When Google created its new social media layer, Google Plus, they used existing Gmail addresses to give users access. The problem for users is that many of them have more than one Gmail address because they were free and became a simple way for people to separate their email. You may have one @gmail.

com for work, another for personal use, and yet another as a junk mail control. Google gives each of those addresses a profile on G+. Whether you're using Google Plus or not, you may have more than one profile sharing your personal information. Claim the right profile(s) in the G+ system so you have control over how you're represented on Google Plus. Even if you never plan to visit again, you should tidy up your real estate.

Currently Google Plus is the second largest social media site. It's 60 percent male and 40 percent female in the United States (more like 70/30 worldwide). There are 300 million active daily users, with the United States leading the way.[13] The demographic is younger on G+ because most of us boomers are not early adopters when it comes to social media. Google Plus users are more technology savvy than Facebook users. While the average G+ user is 28 years old and male, this isn't a reason to disregard the site even if this demographic doesn't contain your ideal prospect. The value of Google Plus is that it's not limited to those already there using the service.

Google Plus is growing so rapidly that some analysts believe Facebook will lose its position at the top in less than five years. I believe it's inevitable that Google Plus will become the number one social networking site on the planet. You need to be there regardless of the demographics at the moment.

Google is the number one search engine in the United States, used by 67 percent of Internet users, so Google controls the majority of what you see when you search for information online.[14] Google decides what content is relevant and what content isn't worth your time. Like it or not, that's the power they hold. Google's mandate is to deliver the most relevant search results.

The news feed or stream of a social media website is your home page. Everyone you connect with while visiting is now your follower, friend, subscriber, or connection. The terminology changes but the relationships are the same. You connect to other people who are sharing messages and having conversations. Their communication will travel down your stream. Likewise, any communication you share will be visible in the news feeds of your followers. This is the public part of a social media destination. There are more private ways to have conversations outside of the mainstream. Not all your conversations have to be public, but it's good to remember that for the most part, everyone can see, hear, and read your messages.

The way Google Plus works is similar to Facebook. You connect with people (called followers) and you can make posts and join groups (called communities), both public and private. You have a news feed where you can see what those you are following have posted, and you can engage with them by commenting on their posts, adding their posts to your news feed, or simply clicking the "+" button to give them a +1 (Google Plus terminology for a thumbs up).

At Google Plus you can follow anyone you like, just as you can on Twitter. You also have the opportunity to organize the people you follow into Circles. Think of them as circles of influence. You can follow as many people, businesses, and communities as you like and categorize them into Circles. This allows you to segment your list by industry, geography, hobbies, or personal interaction. You can place users into more than one Circle, which makes segmenting even easier. This is a feature I wish both LinkedIn and Facebook had.

Google Plus has another cool feature called Hangouts. A Hangout is a videoconference that's free within the platform

and can be either public or private. Another feature available in Hangouts is Hangout On Air, or HOA, where the videoconference broadcasts live to YouTube. You can record the HOA for viewers not present at the time of the live session. Viewers can then watch repeatedly on your YouTube channel. This is a great feature for training sessions within a business, conducting meetings with team members across the globe, or running educational seminars. When more than ten people attend a Hangout, only ten will be on camera "in the room," but hundreds can watch live and interact through a typed chat with the moderator. Best of all, Hangouts are free within Google Plus.

As packed with features as Google Plus is, there's a *bigger* benefit to using the platform: SEO. I mentioned earlier that Google's mandate is to deliver the most relevant search results. So here's what the big G does when you search for something at google.com. It looks at you – peeks over at your G+ profile, sees who's in your Circles, and checks if any of the people or brands in your Circles match your search criteria – then delivers results from Google Plus including posts, communities, and brand pages that match your search query. It's their sandbox, and they do what they can to make sure you keep playing in it.

⭐ Search engine optimization (SEO) is the process of improving the visibility of a website or a web page in a search engine's natural (or unpaid or organic) search results. In general, the earlier (or higher-ranked on the search results page) and more frequently a site appears in the search results list, the more visitors it will receive from the search engine's users. SEO may target different kinds of search, including image search, local search, video search, news search, and industry-specific vertical search engines (Wikipedia 2015).[15]

It's important that you understand that last bit. Google will look at your profile, who you are connected to in Google Plus, and deliver search results based on the connections you have made instead of on what might be most popular across the entire World Wide Web. That means that if you're connected to an ideal prospect in Google Plus, and that prospect searches for goods or services you can deliver, Google is likely to serve up your website before the competition that's not using G+.

CMO.com gives Google Plus a ranking of Good for brand awareness and SEO. At the same time, they rate Google Plus OK for customer service and traffic generation. CMO.com notes that G+ is highly suited for customer service, but consumers haven't figured that out yet. I'm sure they will. To date the platform doesn't generate as much referral traffic as the more established social media sites. Yet CMO.com says, "While Google+ generates less referral traffic, its market share is growing among social media platforms. A recent survey showed referral traffic rose 19 percent from Q3 to Q4 in 2013."

Google Plus is feature-rich and growing at a rapid pace. Google consistently tweaks the environment to make it more useful. The ins and outs of Google Plus are navigable for any business owner, but like all our destinations it will take planning and strategy. It's the most powerful social networking platform in existence. Because of SEO and the sheer size of the Google world, G+ stands to displace Facebook as number one.

Destination: YouTube
What Is It and Who Uses It?

Three former PayPal employees created YouTube, which went live on Valentine's Day 2005. Before you ask . . . yes, YouTube is a social media site, but the primary medium is video rather than images and text. In fact, YouTube has the second largest user population – over one billion monthly active users – behind Facebook. Google saw the potential right away, bought the start-up in 2006, and has been successfully growing it ever since. YouTube is going to be an important part of your business success – and you can find it at www.youtube.com.

Video is a phenomenon that became accessible to everyone because of changes in mobile technology. Every smartphone can be a video camera, which removes the largest barrier to producing video for your business. If you're still not convinced that YouTube is anything other than a place where 18-year-old boys watch Jackass videos and proud parents upload hundreds of hours of cute baby videos, let me clue you in.

According to Google, more than half of the 128 million YouTube visitors per month in the United States are age 35 or over. From an income standpoint, the U.S. visitors to YouTube can be divided by income levels $0–$50,000, $50–$100,000, $100–$150,000, and $150,000 and up. The over $150,000 income range is the largest – 26.5 percent, which I think is important to note given that 26 percent of YouTube visitors are under 18 years old. As far as the male/female ratio, YouTube splits 50/50.[16]

That's who is visiting YouTube; but why are they visiting? There are several reasons, one of which is that YouTube is the second largest search engine, on its own, after Google. In fact, it's bigger than Bing, Yahoo, and ASK combined.[17] This isn't surprising for two reasons: Google, the king of search engines, owns YouTube, and most people are visual learners.  YouTube videos make up 28 percent of all Google search results. Over 90 percent of Internet traffic is video content, and video promotion is six times more effective than print and direct mail promotion. Sixty percent of the visitors to your website will watch the video before reading the text, and they'll stay, on average, two minutes longer on the site after watching a video.[18]

As of this writing YouTube says that users upload 100 hours of video to the site every minute. They reach more people 18–34 years old than any cable network, and 25 percent of the time spent on their site is from a mobile device.[19] There are a lot of cute babies in the world, but let's face it, one of the reasons the quantity of video uploaded every minute has risen exponentially every year is that more and more savvy business owners are using video for marketing.

☛ Users upload 100 hours of video per minute to YouTube. That's over four days worth of video; it's astounding! One in four Internet users in the United States access YouTube monthly. Canadians watch more videos per user than any other country, and YouTube accounts for half of all videos Canadians watch. YouTube reports that 40 percent of its users access the network via a mobile device. There's a tremendous opportunity to market your goods and services on YouTube. Plus, the videos you make available can be shared at other destinations and on websites and blogs.

What makes YouTube a social media site? I'm glad you asked. It's because visitors do more on YouTube than just watch content. Every channel (YouTube's terminology for your real estate on their website) includes videos uploaded to the site, an About section, and a discussion page where viewers can leave comments and interact with your channel. Every video you upload creates an individual page. Viewers leave comments for that single video post, and visitors can give your video a thumbs-up or thumbs-down. Fans show their love by hitting the Subscribe button so they can be alerted every time you upload a new video. This is equivalent to following you on Twitter, friending you on Facebook, or connecting with you on LinkedIn.

Our friends at CMO.com have good things to say about YouTube, although nearly all of YouTube's rankings have lowered from 2013 to 2014. They give the site a rating of OK for every category except customer communication, which they rate as Good. CMO.com notes that the traffic on You-

Tube tends to stay on YouTube, though you can and should include external links to your website or other calls-to-action in the description of your video. The cause for YouTube's decline in other categories boils down to sheer size. YouTube has grown so large that it's become more difficult to get attention. For small business and local business marketing, size doesn't matter. You want to be available 24/7/365 for potential customers, and a YouTube channel is an excellent way to be there and be helpful when your ideal customers need you.

Appendix A has detailed information for opening an account on each of the six social media destinations we have discussed. Included are how-to instructions and details for account set-up, photo sizes required, and other odds and ends to get you started so you'll seem like a local and not a tourist. It will save you time, like an express lane.

What You Need to Know

◆ If you have a Gmail address (or more than one), you most likely already have a Google Plus profile. If your business has a physical address, it most likely already has a Google Plus Business Page.

◆ Facebook and Pinterest are a good place to start if you have a B2C company.

◆ Twitter and LinkedIn are a good place to start if you are a B2B company.

◆ Google Plus and YouTube should be on every business to-do list.

◆ Fill out any social media profile completely and always use high-quality photos where possible on each site, especially for your profile photo.

PART TWO

◆ ◆ ◆ ◆ ◆

Your Survival Guide

CHAPTER FIVE

✦ ✦ ✦ ✦ ✦

Understanding the Language of Social Media

Words and pictures can work together to communicate more powerfully than either alone.

~ WILLIAM ALBERT ALLARD

ONGRATULATIONS! It was hard work, but now you know possibly more than you ever thought you'd know about social media. Understanding the six social media destinations that are most helpful for your business is the first step toward success. Visiting a social media site is like visiting a foreign country. Understanding the language of that country and methods for conveying your marketing message is also critical to your success. So let's look at five steps for crafting the messages you want to share along the itinerary you've chosen to promote your business. These steps are about content – the words, graphics, audio, and video that you'll use in your marketing messages. Following these steps will help you pack the right content, said in a way that everyone can understand. Remember, content is king on the Internet, and on social media it's crucial.

★ On my business podcast, ACT LOCAL Marketing for Small Business, I interviewed business strategist Lisa Manyon, "The Business Marketing Architect." She had a wonderful philosophy based on the adage "content is king." Manyon poses an alternative – content (copy) is queen and strategy is king. Together they're the key to getting results. Manyon's philosophy will serve you well as you learn to create messages that other visitors along your itinerary will understand and enjoy.

One of the mistakes I see baby boomers make when they decide to use social media for marketing is the same mistake many travelers make. Succinctly stated by Mason Cooley, "Travelers never think that they are the foreigners." Too many established business owners think that social media is for advertising. It's free – what a bargain! Then they run out, sign up for accounts at all the hot destinations, and proceed to push out specials and discounts the way they would in a Valpak or PennySaver.

⊗ I've seen many a social media profile opened with the best intentions. Businesses that were intent on being good citizens of the social community, who abandoned those profiles later because they were too difficult to maintain. Yes, social media profiles are free, but using them requires time, effort, and a plan. It's better not to travel to a social media destination, if you don't have time to explore it, than to establish a profile only to abandon it. Account abandonment leaves a terrible impression, and first impressions matter. A link from your website to a Twitter or Facebook page that hasn't been updated in a year will leave a negative impression on your customers who spend time at those destinations.

The truth is, we only believe 14 percent of what a brand tells us through advertising. We have learned to ignore ads, whether on TV, billboards, or the Internet. We are able to compartmentalize what we take in and ignore the stuff we don't want to be bothered with. Using social media to only hawk deals is suicide for any business.

People want to have meaningful, enjoyable, useful, or fun interactions with a brand or business. They don't want coupons, discounts, and deals unless they've specifically asked for them.

Five Steps for Learning to Speak the Language

Below are five steps for learning to speak the language of social media so you will craft the right messages. They are all about content, the stuff you're going to share at each destination. Your message is not just the words you use, but images, audio, and video as well. Content also comes in the form of curating messages other businesses share (curating is when you select content that others have posted on the web and use it to support your message). These are messages that you know your audience will find helpful, even if you didn't create them. These five steps are key to creating a social media strategy that reflects you, your brand, and your business, while making a successful social media strategy possible over the long haul. It's critical that you follow each step to insure that your travels along the digital highway are rewarding.

Language Step 1 – Keep It Simple Stupid

You have probably heard of the KISS principle (Keep It Simple Stupid).[1] KISS is an excellent plan when it comes to social media. Communication in social media and on the Internet in general tends to be disruptive. Razorfish Search says, "Disruptive Communication changes the way consumers talk about a category, a product, or media. It alters consumer perceptions for better or for worse, and it affects the fundamental emotions of the audience. Standing out is achieved as the result of being disruptive in a way that changes or alters a consumer's course of action."[2]

★ People often get upset with the KISS acronym, sometimes dropping the last S in a misguided effort to be politically correct. The U.S. Navy coined the acronym for "Keep it simple stupid" as a design principle for their engineers who designed jets. Most systems work best if they're kept simple. The original phrase has no comma – it's a reminder to keep things stupidly simple to achieve the best result. Others have said the same thing in different ways, such as architect Mies Van Der Rohe, who said "Less is more."

Many messages bombard consumers, who already have short attention spans. More messages being broadcast fosters even shorter attention spans. Conversations jump from site to site and aren't linear or complete, and they often take longer than if the same conversation happened face-to-face. The younger someone is, the less polite they expect a dialogue to be; the opposite is often true for older users. Grammar rules drilled into your head in school no longer apply and can bog down your ability to be heard.

To follow the KISS step, you have to remember that long-winded, formal messages are more likely to be ignored. People are not expecting salutations or a complementary close. Simple statements that leave little room for interpretation are good. Questions are even better. Asking your audience a simple question that generates a simple answer will increase engagement.

For example, if you own a flower shop, don't ask an open-ended question such as, "What types of flowers have you seen in bridal bouquets?" This question has too many potential answers, causing the reader to not bother responding. Rather than take the time to think back on all the flowers they've seen in bridal bouquets – if they were even paying attention enough to notice the flowers in the bridal bouquet – readers will blow right by the question. It's too much effort for them to answer and is unlikely to lead to a dialogue, especially with men. Instead ask, "What's your (or your sweetheart's) favorite color rose?" This simple question suggests a one-word answer, which is what you're looking for. Both men and women are likely to answer, and it's a quick, easy opportunity for engagement. A simple question such as "Roses or Carnations?" will lead to reader interaction and fits with the fast-paced, non-linear communication style that occurs in social media.

People enjoy fill-in-the-blank statements. These are easy to create and gear toward your business brand. Here are some examples:

- My all-time favorite baseball player is (was) __
  _____

- We always eat dinner at _____A.M./P.M.

- Caption this photo: _____

- My Friday night must-have drink is _____

- If I had unlimited funds, I would travel to _____
  _____

- The most popular wedding bouquet flower is __
  _____

The point is to keep it simple and encourage engagement as your message passes by in the endless stream of conversations. Keeping your content simple also limits room for interpretation, especially negative interpretation.

B2B firms often find success with text-only messages that share statistical facts. The wholesale flower distributor can post a message such as, "Men buy 3 out of every 4 of the over 110 million roses sold in the United States every Valentine's Day. Seventy-one percent of those roses are red! What color rose do you find is the favorite at your flower shop on Valentine's Day?" This message provides florists with useful information leading up to Valentine's Day and reminds them to order enough red roses to meet potential demand.

Content is more than just words. It includes images, audio, and video as well, so let's return to the example of "Roses or Carnations?" As a worded question, your followers will understand what you're asking. But instead, you can create an image of a beautiful rose next to an equally beautiful carnation and put "vs." between the two flowers. Better yet, take a photograph of you holding each flower with a questioning look on your face. Do you see how your followers will get the same message? The flower wholesaler can create a similar message with an image of a red rose vs. a bundle of every other color rose and ask which sells more on Valentine's Day.

The image of you asking your readers which flower they prefer is far more personal and engaging than the words themselves. Add to the question with a quick story of why you're asking and people will enjoy engaging in conversation with you. Meanwhile you have conveyed that you're a florist, you sell flowers, your customers' preferences matter to you, and you have knowledge that can help customers make the best choice for their needs. All that communication held in one simple little photo. KISS works in disruptive communication.

Language Step 2 – Keep It Social

After all, it's social media, right? Generally speaking, keeping it social means you want the dialogue to be multi-directional and interactive, not unilateral with you pushing your message out. Marketers call a one-way message a "push" in social media, meaning that you're pushing your agenda onto others. A push message is the sales pitch or discount offer, the one most people skip over and ignore.

⊗ Humor me and answer this question: "Is it easier to push a boulder down a hill or pull it up?" Pushing is faster and easier to do than pulling. Pulling requires more effort over a longer period of time. Pushing the boulders down the hill, however, means that you're building your foundation at the bottom of the hill. Pulling them to the top may take you longer, but you get to build your foundation on top of the hill, where the view is spectacular and more tourists can see you. Your content is the boulder. Will you be pushing it down the hill or pulling it to the top?

"Stop by today for 20% off brown hamsters!" is less likely to get the pet store some business than trying to create a dialogue. Use a message like, "I named my first hamster _____" or post a photo of a hamster from the store doing something crazy or cute and ask people to caption the photo. A one-way message indicates you're not listening. If you're not listening, why should anyone take the time to speak with you? No one enjoys being talked at, even on the Internet.

A better message to share would be tips on the care and feeding of your hamster posted from May 1st through the 9th with a coupon for 20 percent off hamsters on National Hamster Day (May 10th every year, by the way). Include photographs or, better yet, film videos of employees doing the varied tasks required to care for a happy, healthy hamster. This is pushing the boulder up the hill, but you can see how this method is more effective in drawing in potential buyers than just pushing a coupon down the hill and hoping a buyer wanders along and picks it up. Both approaches have the potential to sell hamsters on May 10th. One method may have fleeting success, but the other has laid the foundation for hamster sales beyond National Hamster Day.

Social media has created new ways to engage with your customer. Experts have coined many terms for the subject including *The Thank You Economy,*[3] *relationship marketing, Permission Marketing,*[4] *authentic marketing,* and more. The common theme is your relationship with your customers and the conversations you have with them. The new standard is to build a community, not a soapbox. You want to foster a community, meaning an online center where your ideal prospects and existing customers, clients, and fans can come together and extol your virtues, your brand's virtues, or both. Don't forget, they will also share criticism, but that's good to know too, right? Think of your online community as a favorite tourist shop that everyone knows about and makes a point to stop by when they're in the neighborhood.

When your content reads like you're speaking to your favorite customer, it will resonate more deeply with every visitor because they feel you're speaking directly to them. To help you do this I'll walk you through creating a detailed customer persona in Chapter 9. A customer persona is a representative "person" who is your ideal prospect. Knowing them well will help you craft compelling messages that engage them.

When determining what to share on social media, think of having a conversation with someone. Let them see your expertise in your subject. Show them your passion for your business and other things in your life that matter to you. Think of each piece of content as a one-on-one conversation with your favorite customer rather than a one-to-many unilateral broadcast. You don't strike oil by drilling 100 one-foot-deep wells. You hit oil by drilling just one 100-foot-deep well. Staying social in social media takes time, persistence, research, and planning that in the end will bring greater results.

Language Step 3 – Tell a Story

Stories are incredibly powerful and enduring elements of humankind. Before written language, we told stories to educate, inform, and entertain one another. There are scientific studies in psychology circles that have looked at our penchant for loving a good story.[5] Results of these studies show that our attitudes and values are strongly influenced by the stories we hear. Fiction is a much more effective delivery mechanism for changing people's minds than a well-crafted persuasive essay.

Psychologists tell us that entering a fictional world alters the way we process information. We drop our guard and absorb more information because it's wrapped with emotion. When we're confronted with facts and figures we become analytical, looking for inconsistencies, which keeps our barriers up.

It's easier to influence the outcome of an event by telling a story than by sharing facts and figures – just look to our politicians as an example. The academics who share details using dollar signs and percentage marks to help us understand the gravity of the issues get ignored. They may be absolutely correct in their analyses, but we don't listen with an open heart. The politicians who tell us stories, and weave their "truths" into those stories, capture a nation. They are able to rally the masses and move us to action, even when their "truths" are patently false.

So what is storytelling in marketing? It's the concept that sharing your brand's message through story will have a more powerful and longer-lasting impact than merely sharing facts and figures. Storytelling is used by big brands such as Allstate (Mayhem) or Aflac (the duck), where a character compels us to accept the message. Developing a character for your business that represents what your company stands for is a great idea. The character doesn't have to be physical like Mayhem or the duck. Giving your business brand human characteristics makes it easier for people to understand the mission behind the company.

Take Ben & Jerry's ice cream, for example.[6] The company's mission has always included responsibility for the community and the planet we all share. Its marketing story reflects that in every communication. The company is infused with a humanity that comes across in its marketing story. Its Facebook page lists the company as being in the food and beverage category, but it describes itself this way: "Ben & Jerry's believes business has a responsibility to give back to the community. We make the best possible ice cream in the nicest way possible."

Remember the hamster in our pet store? That pet store could create untold adventures for that hamster and tell those stories a piece at a time to draw us into its world. The store could infuse the hamster with the ideals and characteristics that reflect its business. Those stories will resonate and be memorable. We're highly unlikely to remember when it's "20% off brown hamsters" day unless that little brown hamster makes us care about her.

When developing the story of your business, don't hesitate to include its history, struggles, and triumphs. Allow your story to cultivate a memorable personality that reflects your mission. Don't be reluctant to share the past struggles of your business or your personal story. We love to root for the underdog. We love a heroic journey of success. These are the types of stories that make us feel good. They reveal qualities we'll remember, which will positively influence us and make you stand out in a noisy marketplace. Remember: a good story always has a beginning, a middle, and an end. Like any good novel, every chapter ends with a cliffhanger that makes you want to start reading the next chapter.

Language Step 4 – Make It Scalable

If you're building relationships using social media marketing, the question inevitably arises: how do you scale those relationships (grow them rapidly and at a compound rate)? How do you escalate your conversations? In the real world you can handle only so many friendships, so what's a boomer to do?

Admittedly, it's a difficult question to answer. Scaling usually implies bringing more people into the organization. If you're a small business owner or solo practitioner, hiring may not be a realistic strategy in the beginning. But there are a few things you can do.

Part of the scaling equation is how you interact with the people who are engaging with your business. The type of content you share will help determine your social media scaling strategy. Your content can increase your number of new followers and fans, but also engage those already in your network. For example, if you write every post and start every conversation by teaching or telling a bit of a story, the entire effort rides on your shoulders. You have to be there to create the content consistently, and you have to be there to engage with the followers you are cultivating. If you have the time to devote to that method, great; but most of you have a business to run and grow. If instead you create the type of content that encourages followers to interact with each other that will mean less work for you. That content will foster community and inspire a group dynamic that allows you to spend less time on the social media sites, while still building relationships.

Create quizzes or polls and ask followers to share their results with each other. Help people get the conversation going and then step back and let it go. It's your party, so be a good host. If you've shared your company story, find ways to encourage fans to tell the story for you. Give them open-ended opportunities to share in the narrative. A not-for-profit organization could encourage fans to share their own personal efforts as a continuation of the non-profit's mission. How did that one fan further the cause, raise money, or help others? How is he or she making an impact on his or her small piece of the world? You can find ways and reasons to collaborate with your followers, who then do the scaling for you.

If you have a follower who really likes you, that person may become a brand advocate or evangelist. This is someone who will talk you up to other followers and be a huge asset to you and your business. Cultivating brand advocates furthers your marketing efforts and scales your time commitment because advocates do the work for you. Be on the lookout for followers who frequently speak well of your business and reward them. Let me give you an example.

One of my favorite online tools that helps me with my social media strategy is Buffer (I'll tell you more about what Buffer does and why I like to use it in a later chapter). As a lover of the product, I started attending the company's chat on Twitter, called #BufferChat. On this chat, which happens once a week for an hour like a weekly television show, other brand advocates like me show up and take part in a conversation about something digital-marketing-related. After one of the chats a Buffer employee contacted me privately for my mailing address and sent me a thank you card with Buffer stickers inside. It was a small gesture, but it made me feel special and appreciated. Rewarding brand advocates can be that simple.

A local business can mirror this brand-advocate effort by asking customers to share their stories. Stir the conversation pot. Let your imagination run free. Don't let the type of business you own be a constraint. A dry cleaner could ask customers to talk about the last place they wore a fancy outfit and then share the story. Put up a sign in the store suggesting customers post the story on one of the dry cleaner's social media pages, or post the question as a conversation starter on a site. Take a photo with the customer holding up the fancy duds and post it with the message, "Where was this spectacular dress worn, Susie?" Do a series of posts on how you, the dry cleaner, must handle this type of outfit differently from the norm because of the special beading, stitching, or fabric finish that this particular dress has that makes it fancy.

The travel agent can share customer photos from great vacations and ask customers to share the best _____ (fill in the blank) from their vacations, highlighting categories such as family-friendly, romantic, quiet, or lively locations. The appliance store can ask customers to share favorite family recipes with a photo of them cooking on new appliances bought in their store. Then turn these recipes into a customer cookbook and highlight those customers again and again. The liquor store can share wine pairings from the menu at a recent gala, tagging the patrons and asking for comments. Service-based professionals can share a news story about a topic they deal with daily and ask followers what they think.

Share an idea and ask your audience to embellish it. Encourage dialogue within your community to scale your reach and take some of the burden off you to create content. You can also ask for guest posts and promote them. There are many ways to encourage the members of your community to speak to each other to scale your social media efforts. All the work doesn't have to fall on your shoulders. Remember, as John Heywood said, "Many hands make light work."

If your business has employees, you can share the work. Give staff members a subject or category they can be responsible for and let them be the voice of the business for that topic. Have a social media spokesperson other than yourself who will converse on behalf of your business. For example, you can place someone in charge of customer service (preferably in a proactive fashion), sales generation, or prospect nurturing, while you find, attract, and focus on the prospects you think are ideal. Be willing to ask your staff for help.

☛ Placing someone else in charge of social media requires you to create guidelines for them to follow. They need to know how to speak on behalf of you and your business. How to create such a guide is a topic I'll discuss in more detail in an upcoming chapter. Just a heads up for now: if you are thinking about a specific employee who would be perfect for the task, that person will need some extra guidance that you will have to provide.

Language Step 5 – Have a Social Media Strategy

The fifth and final step is having a strategy. You must consider what needs to be a part of your social media strategy before you can put together a MAP, or marketing action plan, to serve as your roadmap to using social media for business growth.

You can find thousands of articles online about building a social media strategy. You don't need to reinvent the wheel. Research how other businesses have used social media successfully to fuel your creative engine. You'll save time in the long run if you learn how to be successful from the start. There are common threads among these articles, and the upcoming chapters cover most of these threads in some detail. For now, here's a short summary of some of the common aspects of successful social media marketing strategies.

First, define your goals. Why are you considering social media as a marketing tool in the first place? There are plenty of good reasons to use social media for marketing, just make sure you define the specific goals for your business. For example, are you looking to build a following nationally, regionally, or locally? Is social media a way to bring visitors to your website? Do you have a movement that you're trying to perpetuate? Are you seeking sponsors for your cause or business? Be thoughtful and define a handful of goals that are clearly identified for your business.

Second, know your audience. Creating the ideal prospect persona will help. To do this effectively, you need to understand your prospects' biggest goals and challenges and how you can help them achieve those goals or overcome those challenges.

You'll also want to determine which social media sites your clients already spend time on. You can explore the Internet on your own and look at their behavior, or you can simply ask them if they frequent Facebook, Twitter, LinkedIn, Pinterest, Google Plus, or YouTube. Asking them can

Speak the Language of Social Media

KEEP IT SIMPLE STUPID

KEEP IT SOCIAL

TELL A STORY

MAKE IT SCALABLE

HAVE A SOCIAL MEDIA STRATEGY

save time in deciding which destination to visit first and save resources when attempting to reach them. By asking them which destinations they visit most often in the social media world, you'll already be taking one step toward engaging them in your efforts.

Start with the site that has the largest concentration of your market prospects. If prospects are on a site you're not familiar with, or haven't visited yourself, invest the time and effort to learn more about that site. Resist the temptation to default to another site that's more familiar to you. It makes sense to go where the customers are, otherwise you're likely wasting your time, and that's a precious resource you can never get back. Knowing our six destinations already gives you a leg up. Look at visiting someplace new as an adventure rather than a chore. You may discover you love visiting that site.

Consider choosing some hot-button topics in your market. These are subjects people are talking about in your field of expertise, the things they never seem to get tired of discussing. These hot buttons will create themes for you to build content around.

Third, make the effort to use a vanity URL. A URL, or Uniform Resource Locator, is an address on the Internet. An example of a vanity URL is www.NewYorkTimes.com, which takes you to *The New York Times* online. It's a good idea to keep your URLs consistent across all your social media websites. For example, if your company is XYZ Corporation, you want your Facebook URL to be www.facebook.com/xyzcorp. Try to find a vanity name that you can use everywhere. If your company name is taken by someone else on Facebook but not Twitter, do your best to come up with a name you can use on both sites. This is where some homework is required. Test your ideal vanity name at all six destinations and see if it's available; then adjust as necessary. Keeping a URL the same on all social media sites makes it easier for followers to find you at each destination and for the conversation to bounce around.

Fourth, include measurement in your social media strategy. How many miles per gallon are you getting on this trip? In other words, how much mileage are you getting out of your social media strategy? You need to have a plan in place to measure your results at each social media destination – that is, whether or not you've met your social media goals. This tells you if your efforts are having the desired effect, also referred to as a positive ROI (return on investment). Remember, you can't measure ROI without first having specific goals. Also, each of the elements of your social media strategy discussed above should work in concert.

What You Need to Know

- We only believe 14 percent of what a brand tells us through advertising. Social media is not free advertising.

- Social media content is multi-directional. Your content should encourage conversation, unlike one-way messages (advertisements), which don't.

- Treat every piece of content as a one-on-one conversation with your favorite customer rather than a one-to-many broadcast.

- Giving your business human characteristics makes it easier for people to understand the mission behind the company (like the Aflac duck or Mr. Clean).

- Cultivating brand advocates scales your social media marketing efforts.

- You need to determine why you want to use social media marketing and then develop goals based on that determination. You want to be able to determine your ROI (return on investment). Take some measurements initially and track them over time.

CHAPTER SIX

❖ ❖ ❖ ❖ ❖

Learning Social Media Etiquette

Communities do not work unless they are regulated by etiquette.

~ JUDITH MARTIN (MISS MANNERS)

E HAVE DISCUSSED what to say in social media; now let's look at how to say it. Social media websites have various etiquette standards that users take *very seriously*. Violating these standards can leave new visitors out in the cold. How you share your marketing message can make or break your social media success.

This area of the MAP is about communication, and it covers four standards that your unique marketing message should include. Using these standards will have you blending in like a native. Your communication style is simply the way you share information through language, both written and spoken. In social media messages, your voice – or the voice of your business – has to come through in an identifiable way. The development of that voice can make you stand out in a noisy crowd.

Let me start by stating the obvious: men and women communicate differently. But not all men fit their communication stereotype, and not all women fit theirs. Knowing whether you're speaking to men or women may be helpful in choosing your words, but in general you shouldn't get caught up in making that distinction. Unless you have niched down so far within your market that you know your ideal prospects all fit the same mold and respond to a specific communication style, don't sweat it. Develop your unique voice and it will resonate with your ideal customers.

There have been many studies done on communication, and it seems there are often two continuums that cross: one is assertiveness and the other is responsiveness. The assertiveness scale runs from highly assertive to highly cooperative, and the cross scale runs from highly responsive to highly passive. Another way to think of them is direct versus indirect and competitive versus collegial. We all fall somewhere on these two continuums and where you fall will determine your communication style.

You may decide that, given your brand's persona, your personal communication style isn't right for your brand. You'll have to adapt how you communicate to appeal to your target market. Exhibit 6.1 shows a matrix of traits associated with each communication style. See which traits describe you and which should describe your business, and then make adjustments.

Except for video, on social media the people you communicate with cannot see you. They are absorbing your communication in words and images without the influence of body language, context, or knowledge of your communication style. A cooperative, collegial type of person may not enjoy an assertive and competitively styled message. While I don't want you to get all crazy about this stuff, you do need to

COMMUNICATION STYLES / TRAITS

		LOW ← **ASSERTIVENESS** → HIGH	
		COOPERATIVE (asks) • Lots of information used • Process-oriented and people-oriented	**ASSERTIVE** (tells) • Little information used • Action-oriented and idea-oriented
HIGH ← **RESPONSIVENESS** → LOW	**COMPETITIVE** (self-controlled) • Creates change • Task-oriented	**Analytical Traits** • Problem solver • Factual • Consistent • Accurate • Cautious • Sensitive • Perfectionist • Critical • Scheduled • Organized • Orderly • Persistent • Logical • Detailed • Impersonal • Inquisitive • Picky	**Driver Traits** • Goal-driven • Independent • Action-oriented • Competitive • Purposeful • Serious • Strong-willed • Practical • Takes charge • Seeks power • Persistent • Controlling • Self-reliant • Productive • Firm • Judges quickly • Efficient
	COLLEGIAL (shows emotion) • Provides choice • Relationship-oriented	**Amiable Traits** • Enjoys popularity • Sympathetic • Calm • Nurturing • Cooperative • Personal • Respectful • Reserved • Loyal • Adaptable • Dry humor • Tolerant • Patient • Good listener • Thoughtful • Enjoys routine	**Influencer Traits** • Enthusiastic • Fun-loving • Intuitive • Creative • Optimistic • Takes risks • Promotes • Emotional • Inspirational • Spontaneous • Likes variety • Enjoys change • Ambitious • Friendly • Energetic • Group-oriented • Animated

think it over for the sake of your business, because your followers will pick up the underlying tones and feelings within your communication. My favorite Maya Angelou quote is, "I've learned that people will forget what you said, people will forget what you did, but people will never forget how you made them feel." This is a good mantra to keep in mind when communicating on social media. The feelings you create with your message will linger the longest.

As you build your social media MAP, you determine where to visit, what to say, and how to say it. Now you're ready to incorporate four plans for communicating that will have you following standards of social media etiquette and blending in like a native.

Etiquette Plan 1 – Be Accessible

The whole point of social media is to be social. Businesses that push out messages and never check to see how fans and followers respond are missing the point. People who use social media to engage with brands do it because they like the content or the company or both, not just because they like receiving discount coupons – although they might like that too. People enjoy participating in contests and sweepstakes online, and they like having the opportunity to use social media for customer service-related issues. Of course, that last one only works if your business is responsive and accessible on a regular basis. Responding to a customer service issue a week later is doing more harm than good. Followers like to share, with other members of the community, any experiences they have with a product or service. Social media takes word of mouth to the nth degree. That's why it's important for you to maintain an accessible social media profile for your business.

Kalynn Amadio - "The Boomer Gal"
Host ACT LOCAL Marketing Podcast
Boomer's Ultimate Guide Podcast
T. 914-409-9009 • ka@theboomergal.com
ACTLOCALmarketing.com • TheBoomerGal.com

★ Your email signature can be set to display more than just "Regards." It's a common practice and a great idea to put links to your social media pages directly after your name in the signature portion of your email. See how mine looks above.

Be accessible offline, too, with these simple tricks. Make sure your clients and customers know where to find your business on social media sites by printing the vanity URLs of your social media business pages on promotional materials. Put up posters and signs around your brick-and-mortar location reminding people where to find you online. Encourage them to visit you all along your chosen itinerary. Put links to those destinations on your business card and in your email signature. Don't be shy about letting people know where you are. You've decided that social media is part of building your business, so put it to good use by being accessible.

Etiquette Plan 2 – Be Transparent

This one scares some businesses (and governments). Transparency is a trait we value in communication but rarely receive. All too often we analyze to determine where the lies are, thinking, "How is this deal going to screw me?" We cannot help but look for the negative because our guard is up. Whether it's business or government, we fear that we're not getting the whole truth, so we become distrustful.

Part of the blame lies in advertising. Advertising has always been about how to create want and get people to buy; whether people needed what was being sold was irrelevant. Boomers who jump on the social media bandwagon often treat it as a source of free advertising. See the inherent problem? We don't trust advertising, so we don't trust businesses that only advertise to us. Social media isn't for advertising – it's for conversation. Allowing interactions to be transparent will set you apart from businesses that only push messages out.

Giving your social media followers a clear view into your business is another approach that builds trust. When prospects know, like, and trust you, they'll buy from you and become customers for life. There is great value in a lifetime customer, so be transparent.

⊗ Being transparent doesn't mean exposing your warts. Sharing behind-the-scenes peeks into your business is alluring and engages a strong following, but don't share anything that makes you feel uncomfortable or that your gut tells you is a bad idea – listen to your internal voice. Hot-button topics such as politics and religion will always create strong feedback. Try not to start or engage in conversations about subjects that have nothing to do with your business unless you're prepared to stand your ground and possibly lose business.

We can't help wanting a peek behind the curtain. Use this innate sense of curiosity we all have to your advantage by being transparent. Post photos of a new product shipment that you're excited about before it hits the shelves. Celebrate an employee birthday or other milestone with your followers. Make followers feel they're part of the family and they'll become loyal advocates.

Etiquette Plan 3 – Be Consistent

Consistency is the first thing to go when the going gets tough. How many Facebook pages and Twitter accounts have you run across that have no updates in months or years? I see them all the time, and I make an immediate judgment about that business.

The thing about consistency is that you get to decide what consistent means. If maintaining a consistent social media strategy means that you post on Facebook every Wednesday, then make darn sure you post every Wednesday. Your fans will begin to anticipate your new content. You create an expectation, but then you must stick with it. That's why planning upfront will be helpful to you in the long run.

⊗ Businesses that jump in and try to do it all without a plan end up overwhelmed and floundering, and they ultimately pull the plug on social media. Figure out a consistent schedule that's workable from the beginning. You can always increase engagement as your strategy matures or when you get a larger team behind you.

Using social media to market your business is like the story of the tortoise and the hare. Steady, consistent growth takes time and dedication and leads to success. There are ways to sprint like a hare, but they're not sustainable in the long run. To grow your social media reach and have positive outcomes, you must be consistent. There's no other way. I'm going to teach you some tricks that make consistency less of an issue as you travel along the digital highway.

Etiquette Plan 4 – Be Influential

The fourth plan of engagement in our MAP is to be influential. Becoming an influential voice doesn't happen overnight, unless you already have an offline reputation that will attract people to communicate with you online. I'm a firm believer that everyone is an expert at something. Chances are you're an expert in one or more aspects of your business. It's this expertise that will grant you influence online.

It's far easier for you to share the things you already know than to try and learn new things, so start with what you know. Showcase your knowledge by giving it away. Being helpful and generous is highly appreciated in social media. I cannot stress that point enough. We hold generosity in high esteem in social media. The more you share your expertise, the more of an expert you become online. This will build your credibility and your community.

Giving things away for free is a difficult concept for boomers in business. It's not how your mentors taught you to handle business. But here's the thing: knowledge is power. People don't know what knowledge you own until you share it. You probably know more about your particular field of expertise than you could ever share.

Sit down and answer the ten most frequently asked questions you see in your business. That alone will give you weeks' or months' worth of shareable content. Then answer the ten questions your ideal prospects should be asking you if they knew enough about your product, service, or industry to understand what to ask. Those answers are splendid content to share. Between the ten frequently-asked questions (FAQ) and the ten should-ask questions (SAQ), you'll have a huge variety of information that your social media followers will love receiving. This returns us to the "know, like, and trust" factors. You're building relationships with people. The more expertise you showcase, the more influential you become.

Answering FAQ and using those answers as content in social media serves another purpose. It does work for you around the clock by removing obstacles for potential customers who are on the fence about doing business with you. When you provide clients with answers to their questions up front, you are showing transparency and a greater understanding of their needs. That builds influence. You should plan to promote FAQ content on a regular basis. It's not enough to assume that because you said it once, everyone got it. Find multiple ways to answer the same questions. They're frequent for a reason; don't feel self-conscious about repeating yourself. Some things need repeating on a consistent basis.

What You Need to Know

◆ Every social media site is like a foreign country. You will get along much better if you understand the etiquette.

◆ Know your communication style and whether it's right for the public communications of your business or brand. A warm and fuzzy brand cannot use militarily precise language. It will only confuse customers and turn them away.

◆ One key to a successful social media strategy is *accessibility*. This is especially appreciated as a customer service function.

◆ The more you share your expertise, the more of an expert you become online. This will build your credibility and your community.

CHAPTER SEVEN

* * * * *

Transporting Content and Time Management

For time is the longest distance between two places.

~ TENNESSEE WILLIAMS

AT THIS STAGE IN THE PLANNING PROCESS you've done most of the hard work. You've researched where you're most likely to find ideal prospects who have money to spend. You've learned what type of message to share at each social media destination on your itinerary. Because you know how to communicate in a way that resonates with your customers and ideal prospects, your social media profiles are poised to become popular tourist destinations that receive frequent visitors.

The next two parts of the MAP are closely related. There are alternatives you need to understand and consider when it comes to delivering your marketing messages on social media – three basic methods of transport and two time management roads to follow (as a busy boomer it's in your best interest to be effective at getting your messages out in a timely manner).

Methods of Transport

First let's look at your three choices for transporting or delivering your content to its destination social media site. It ain't rocket science, but it requires some thought because choosing the right method of transport will ensure that your social media marketing is effective. A successful company has systems in place for all aspects of the business, and this includes social media marketing. The first transport option to consider is hand delivery.

Transport Option 1 – Hand Delivery

The most common method to start getting your messages into various social media channels is by hand-delivering them. You're learning about each social media website on your itinerary, how it works, who hangs out there, and what kind of conversations resonate with other visitors. By hand-delivering your content you learn to post, tweet, pin, and plus your way through the landscape like a native.

Hand delivery means you are sharing content and listening for feedback in real time. When you receive comments on your messages, you respond to them personally. You maintain your news feed on time. Fielding friend requests, following and unfollowing other visitors, checking out communities and groups at each destination, and joining the countless conversations happening around town are how you spend your time at each spot on the MAP.

Transport Option 2 - Automated Delivery

Hand delivery is great in many ways because it gives every conversation a personal touch, but eventually it becomes too time consuming. As your network grows, you won't be able to keep up with the demands of in-person delivery. This is where automation becomes helpful.

You can automate your social media marketing delivery by using third-party software – most commonly through the use of web applications. These tools allow you to manage your existing social media account profiles from one web location – you can easily upload your marketing content to this single location where it will be delivered to all your social media accounts automatically.

Third-party tools are enormously helpful in managing the delivery of your content and minimizing the time it takes you to make those deliveries. Some popular tools are Hootsuite (www.hootsuite.com) and my personal favorite, Buffer (www.bufferapp.com). There are other, more-robust solutions, for larger businesses with complex social media marketing needs, known as SMMS or Social Media Management System tools. If you need this level of help, check out Buddy Media (part of Salesforce.com), Virtue (part of Oracle.com), or Engage121 (www.engage121.com).

These tools also have built-in scheduling capability, which means that you can upload a day's or week's worth of content at one time and schedule the exact date and time you want the content shared with your followers. By scheduling your message delivery you'll save an immense amount of time as your social network grows.

What automation cannot do is respond to comments or engage in real-time conversation. You can automate outgoing messages but not responses to incoming messages.

A common mistake small businesses make in the beginning is automating their social media output without checking for feedback. It's a mistake because the conversational aspect of social media is ignored. I'll say it again – social media is about communication, which includes responding to conversations initiated by your fans and followers. To respond, you have to be listening. When all your social media networking exchanges are nothing but pushed-out messages that encourage no interaction, they are no different from advertising. More advertising? No thanks; we don't want it. We want conversation.

(X) Local residents have a short tolerance for automated social media feeds that show no personal interaction. Relying on 100 percent automation is a sure-fire way to sabotage your trip before it's even begun to get interesting. In the long run it's a waste of time to "set it and forget it."

Transport Option 3 – A Blend of Both

The best option for delivering your brand's content is a blend of both modes of transport: hand delivery and automated delivery. This combination should become your permanent system. Ideally you'll develop a process to create the content you share and then load the majority of that content into third-party scheduling tools. Part of your strategy will include scheduling time to check each destination website to see if any of your visitors have made comments on your content. You can then respond in a variety of ways available at each location.

On the six social media sites we've covered, people can make comments about your content, and you, in turn, can respond to those comments. There are other ways to engage your followers and visitors depending on where you are. At Facebook, for example, you can "Like" a comment to let the speaker know you saw what he or she had to say and that you felt his or her input was worthy of a thumbs-up. Twitter has a function that lets you acknowledge a comment in your news feed stream (known as a re-tweet), or you can "Favorite" a comment, which gives it a gold star and automatically places it on a special list on your home page.

On Pinterest, you can click the "Heart" button, which means you have some love for a pin. Google Plus has created a system that adds a new vocabulary to our dictionary. On G+ you can give a post or comment a "+1," much the same as a "Like" thumbs-up at Facebook. In nearly every circumstance there's a quick-click way to interact with every piece of content shared and every comment left so that your friends and followers see your interaction. Every comment doesn't need a verbal response on your part, but people do appreciate when you take the time to converse and push the conversation forward. One-to-one interaction increases popularity.

Time Management

After choosing a method of transport for delivering your content, you'll find that you need to choose one of two roads to make the delivery in a way that makes the best use of your time. For our purposes this is also known as time management. In the beginning it's important to engage with other visitors in person so you can learn the language, etiquette, and culture of each destination on your itinerary. If you find the best spots to frequent, you'll get the most bang for your buck. Once you have a good understanding of each site, you can choose how you want to automate. Let me show you some shortcuts along the two possible roads you can take to manage your time efficiently.

Time Management Road 1 – Do It Yourself

When Dorothy wondered where to start her journey on the yellow brick road, the Munchkins said, "It's usually best to start at the beginning." The beginning in this case means you do the journey yourself, so you get to know the landscape in order to build a strong foundation for your strategy.

Depending on your budget, the do-it-yourself approach may be the most reasonable for a long time. Who knows? You may discover you like social media! Blocking out time on a daily and weekly basis to keep your social media strategy fine-tuned is your best bet. It is a good idea to use an actual timer so that you're in control of your time. Social media, like the Internet in general, can swallow large chunks of your time if you don't keep your wits about you. I recommend spending a minimum of 30 minutes every day like this:

Daily Schedule

- **Facebook – 6 minutes:** Respond to any comments made on your content from the day before. Scroll through your news feed and "Like" the content and comments of other people and businesses you follow. Post your content for the day on your business page.

- **Twitter – 8 minutes:** Respond to any tweets sent directly to you or that include you. Scroll through your Twitter feed or list and choose a few pieces of content tweeted by thought leaders and influencers in your industry, then re-tweet and respond to them. Post your content for the day. Follow 10 percent more people each day and return follow-worthy tweeters.

♦ **LinkedIn – 6 minutes:** Share your content for the day. Visit one group and share your content. Engage in any conversation that you find notable in a group. Accept or ignore connection requests and reply to messages.

♦ **Pinterest – 4 minutes:** Pin your content for the day. Scroll through the feed and "Heart" or re-pin anything that you find notable. Leave a comment on something you find engaging.

♦ **Google Plus – 6 minutes:** Respond to any notifications on your content from the day before. Share your new content for the day. Visit one community and share your content. Engage in any conversation that you find notable in a community. Follow and/or follow back new people who interest you. Comment on content shared by a thought leader in your industry.

These times are a guide, not a hard and fast rule, to keep you from getting sucked into the social media vacuum. Set your timer and do as many of these things each day as you can within the time you've allotted. Then move on. Literally stand up and walk away from the computer when your timer goes off. Spend five minutes filling your lungs with fresh air, refill your coffee mug, and go on with your day. This schedule is an example of how you can visit all destinations in one day.

You noticed that I didn't include YouTube in your daily interaction. If you are using YouTube, you'll typically need a very large following before you'll see other users commenting on your videos. For businesses, video on YouTube is a way to showcase expertise – the videos themselves don't garner many comments. It's okay to check weekly for YouTube comments. If you discover your videos are receiving lots of attention, rearrange your time to check in more often. YouTube is also connected to Google Plus, so your comments and +1s on Google+ videos (which are YouTube videos) will show up on YouTube and vice versa.

I recommend spending 30–45 minutes once a week doing the following:

Weekly Schedule

♦ Decide what content subject(s) you'll share that week and track down appropriate articles at online news and magazine outlets published in the past week. Copy and paste the addresses of the articles into a document or spreadsheet for reference during the week.

♦ Find or create images that support your subject(s) – at least one for each day that you'll be posting. You can use this image on more than one site. Do any editing required to make the image unique to your business.

♦ Look for one to three inspirational quotes that are appropriate for your content and business that week. Quotes continue to be very popular on social media.

♦ Check each social media site for thought leaders in your industry and follow them. Make a note in your spreadsheet of their names so you can look for them in order to re-share or comment on their content during the week. A good place to start is the author of an article you chose to share.

♦ If you're using YouTube, post your latest video for the week. Answer any comments that appeared during the previous week and subscribe to a thought leader in your industry. Leave a comment on one of his or her videos.

☛ Here is one of my favorite cheats to find content worth sharing. Even though you create some of the content you share about your business, a large part of your content sharing will be images and articles created by others. A super timesaver technique to track down articles is to sign up for website newsletters from publications or people who consistently write about your industry. Many large companies scour the Internet for relevant information to share with their readers. Let the big guys do the work for you and have it delivered to your mailbox. Then you can choose the articles each week that you want to share in your social media feed in a fraction of the time it would take you to find them on your own. That's a super-duper top secret you can thank me for when we run into each other online!

That's it! If you're only using one social media site to build your business, then of course you can spend less than 30 minutes per day. Better yet, you can spend the entire 30 minutes and dive deep at one site, making more connections and engaging more strongly with that community. You can make adjustments to the weekly curation work as well – curate content for two weeks at a time or a month at a time, if that works for you. The important point is to block time on your schedule and use a timer to stay on track. This is a journey, like the tortoise and the hare. As long as you remain consistent, results will follow.

That was the first fork of your two road choices. Once your successful efforts expand beyond your time allowance, you have new decisions to make. The second road is to give this work to someone else to do for you.

Time Management Road 2 – Outsource It

Outsourcing the delivery of your content makes a lot of sense, but you need to put some things in place before traveling that road. First you'll need a social media policy and style guide. This document is the step-by-step guide you provide to the team doing the work for you. It's your training manual for using social media in your business.

We discussed the social media style guide in detail in Chapter 6. It's the voice and persona of your business brand – the way your brand "sounds" when it speaks, whom you are speaking with, and how often you engage in conversation. A social media policy is different – it outlines your expectations and rules for employee communication. This includes not just communicating online, as a representative of your business, but also communicating in public, where the employee is known to work for your business.

Fortunately, you don't have to reinvent the wheel when creating your policy because there are many examples available online for you to adjust and use.[1] Here are some noteworthy samples.[2]

1. **Kodak and its transparency guidelines:** "Even when you are talking as an individual, people may perceive you to be talking on behalf of Kodak. If you blog or discuss photography, printing, or other topics related

to a Kodak business, be upfront and explain that you work for Kodak; however, if you aren't an official company spokesperson, add a disclaimer to the effect: 'The opinions and positions expressed are my own and don't necessarily reflect those of Eastman Kodak Company.'"

2. **Intel and its moderation guidelines:** "The Good, the Bad, but not the Ugly. If the content is positive or negative and in context to the conversation, then we approve the content, regardless of whether it's favorable or unfavorable to Intel. However, if the content is ugly, offensive, denigrating, and completely out of context, then we reject the content."

3. **IBM and its value guidelines:** "If it helps you, your coworkers, our clients or our partners to do their jobs and solve problems; if it helps to improve knowledge or skills; if it contributes directly or indirectly to the improvement of IBM's products, processes and policies; if it builds a sense of community; or if it helps to promote IBM's Values, then it is adding value. Though not directly business-related, background information you choose to share about yourself, such as information about your family or personal interests, may be useful in helping establish a relationship between you and your readers, but it is entirely your choice whether to share this information."

A social media policy serves as a base for your expectations concerning online communications, but it also empowers others to speak for your business on your behalf. It's an important step to take if you're going to outsource social media to get it done.

You can outsource the work by training an employee based on all of the decisions you made while crafting a social media strategy. Or you can offload the work to an outside digital marketing firm to handle. Either way you'll need to have a plan in place – a map, or in our case a MAP.

What You Need to Know

◆ Hand delivery is personal. It has you knocking on doors and meeting the people you want to speak with, but it takes time and it's difficult to scale.

◆ Automated delivery solves the scaling problem, but it's impersonal and more likely to be ignored over time, thwarting your marketing efforts.

◆ Social media can be like quicksand when it comes to your time, sucking you in and causing you to lose time that's better spent in other ways. Having a daily and weekly schedule will keep you from getting sucked in, and it will make using social media for marketing an effective strategy.

◆ Outsourcing, or having someone else do the traveling and posting for you, is viable, but you need to have parameters in place first or you won't get the results you seek.

CHAPTER EIGHT

Managing Your Sharing Frequency and Measuring Success

What gets measured gets managed.

~ PETER DRUCKER

YOU ARE WELL ON THE WAY to creating and implementing a successful social media marketing strategy. While it would be great to get going and have some fun traveling, there's one last piece of the plan that you need to consider – the numbers. A successful trip has a schedule and budget to keep it on track. There are rules of the road to consider in every social media strategy, such as frequency of engagement. Say too much and nobody wants to listen. Say too little and nobody hears you through the noise. And finally, the way to determine if your strategy is working is the use of metrics – deciding what to measure so you can manage your efforts and make changes to your itinerary as necessary.

Ideal Sharing Frequencies

How often you share content with your audience will fluctuate as you get your social media program up and running. Some social media sites, such as Facebook and YouTube, have built-in analytics tools to make getting information about your followers easy. Here are some rules of thumb to use as benchmarks to begin with (all times are local to you):

Facebook: Share up to three times per day, but no more. Start with morning, afternoon, and evening, then watch to see which posts and what times are the most popular. Experts suggest the ideal post arrival time to be between 1:00 P.M. and 4:00 P.M.

Twitter: Share between eighteen and twenty-four tweets per day. Power users will post over forty tweets per day, but there are diminishing returns, so it's not worth the time to post beyond twice an hour. Experts suggest that the ideal tweet arrival time is between 1:00 P.M. and 3:00 P.M., so I recommend that, in the beginning, you save your most important tweets for that window of time.

LinkedIn: Share no more than two to three posts per day in your general feed. Every time you post new content inside a group that activity also appears in your general feed, so it's redundant if done at the same time as a general post. Try posting one to two times in the morning and once in the evening. Experts suggest that the ideal post arrival time is between 7:00 A.M. and 9:00 A.M. and 5:00 P.M. and 6:00 P.M.

Pinterest: It's okay to post as often as you like on Pinterest, but it's best to spread your posts throughout the day to catch maximum audience. Experts suggest that the ideal post arrival time is between 2:00 P.M. and 4:00 P.M. and again between 8:00 P.M. and 1:00 A.M.

Google Plus: Share as often as you feel inspired on Google Plus. You'll find that your engagement is highest at different times on different days, but experts suggest that the ideal post arrival time is between 9:00 A.M. and 11:00 A.M. daily.

YouTube: Share any number of videos you feel inspired to create. If you're setting up a television show-style format, post your video at the same time every day or week, just as television programs are telecast. YouTube viewer traffic is heaviest from 11:00 A.M. to 5:00 P.M. weekdays, with Wednesday and Thursday seeing slightly more traffic.

Measuring Social Media Success

This is probably the most overlooked and least frequently done part of any social media MAP. Not measuring the results of your social media activities is equal to not doing regular maintenance on your vehicle. Metrics are necessary if you want your plan to run smoothly, and they provide you with the feedback you need to make informed decisions. You need metrics to increase the return on investment from using social media to grow your business.

I mentioned that most social media sites have built-in analytics tools that give you a general sense, at a glance, which content you've shared is making an impact. Facebook, for example, has a tool called Insights. On the Insights dashboard you can quickly see the total number of Likes your business page has earned, weekly total reach (number of people who have potentially seen the content) of your Facebook page, and the engagement your posts have received from followers. Insights also gives you a breakdown per post so you can see which content posts were the most popular so you create more like them.

Keep in mind, the time of day you posted your more popular content may also be playing a factor in its popularity. Also, don't be discouraged by low percentages. Facebook says that, on average, only 16 percent of your fans will be reached organically by your page content. Keep that benchmark in mind. Facebook is hoping that to reach more than 16 percent, you'll pay them to boost your posts, which is another strategy you can use, budget permitting.

The YouTube analytics dashboard can tell you how many views each video you've uploaded received, the number of likes or dislikes per video, number of minutes watched, number of subscribers to your channel, shares on other social media of your videos, how many embeds your videos have garnered (embed = inserting a video into another web page), and much more. The analytics at YouTube are extensive, which makes sense since Google owns YouTube. That leads us to your next step in metrics.

A useful tool in keeping and reporting metrics is Google Analytics. It's another one of the free resources Google offers businesses to gauge how their digital marketing efforts are working. There's more data gathered, stored, and available on Google Analytics than you may ever figure out how to use. One of its most useful metrics tracks traffic from anywhere on the Internet to your website, including social media website traffic, and that can help you better understand the effectiveness of your efforts.

You can open a Google Analytics account with your Gmail address and place the required code on your web pages. Google will then begin tracking activity on your website. Once you have some data stored, navigate to the Traffic

Sources > Social > Overview tab for a look at where your social media-related website traffic is coming from. You should track whether these numbers rise through your MAP efforts.

☛ Google Analytics is a helpful tool to incorporate into your website. When you sign up for a free Analytics account and register your website, Google gives you a piece of code that has to be placed on your web pages. That code runs in the background and collects data for you to review. If you're using WordPress, there's a plugin called SEO for WP by Yoast that's excellent. It gives you a place to insert the code, which takes care of the whole issue. Several WordPress themes also make integration of Google Analytics easy. If the word *code* is making you sweat and you're already thinking this is too much, never fear – you can visit a site called eLance.com, where freelance coders will bid to do the job for you for anywhere from $10 to $30. If you feel tech savvy, just use Google search to find articles on how to insert the code on your exact type of website. You can even ask your hosting service provider to take care of it for you. Many will give you instructions or do it for you for nothing.

Another metric to tell you if your social media marketing efforts are having an impact is social influence, measured by your Klout score. Klout is a website (www.klout.com) that also allows you to set up a free account and connect your social media profiles to it. Klout then tracks the interactions you generate with other community members of the social media destinations you frequent. Without getting into the politics involved in the use of Klout (and, believe me, there are politics involved among heavy social media users), it's a good method to see if your efforts are having the desired impact. In essence, you'll be able to determine, to an extent, if your engagement on the various social media sites is raising your clout (Klout) in the community. Are you gaining social influence? If not, then you can tweak your efforts by engaging more often with other travelers and promoting your business less. No engagement and constant self-promotion are telltale signs that you have no clout . . . I mean Klout. There are many other social influence measurement tools you can use – check out Kred, Peerindex, and Tweetreach.

It's never wrong to keep track of how many Followers, Likes, Retweets, Repins, Shares, +1s, and Embeds happen with your content. An increasing trend in any of these numbers is always a good sign, but it doesn't give you the whole picture. You want people to engage with your content and heed your call to action. If your social media MAP efforts are moving traffic, but nothing happens once visitors reach your website, you'll need to look at that part of the mix next. The purpose of your website is to get a visitor to take action.

Now let's jump in and get you moving along the digital highway.

What You Need to Know

♦ How often you share content varies by destination and is part of the accepted etiquette practiced at each social media site.

♦ All six social media destinations have built-in analytics for business pages.

♦ Choose what metrics you're going to track to determine if your MAP is succeeding, and use analytics to watch growth.

♦ Install Google Analytics on your website to view the social sites that send you the most referral traffic.

◆ ◆ ◆ ◆ ◆

CHAPTER NINE

How to Get the Most Out of This Book

By failing to prepare, you are preparing to fail.

~ BENJAMIN FRANKLIN

MANY PEOPLE DON'T GET THIS FAR, so what you should do now is acknowledge your perseverance. (A pat on the back is appropriate.) Planning isn't the most fun part of social media marketing for the majority of business owners. Those who do manage to plan don't think through all the action steps. Having a plan is necessary, but as Eisenhower said, "In preparing for battle I have always found that plans are useless, but planning is indispensable."

Now you're ready for the next leg of your journey. You have all the information you need to make a personalized MAP (Marketing Action Plan) to take you from where you are now to where you want to go on the digital highway. Your plan will be your guide to meeting ideal prospects, building relationships, and turning those prospects into paying customers through the smart use of social media. Your MAP will look something like the one shown on the next page.

M.A.P. (MARKETING ACTION PLAN)

Choose Itinerary (circle one)
On The Street: B2C
Enterprise: B2B
Crossroads: Mix

Step 1: Who Is My Customer
Build Your Ideal Customer Avatar
_____
_____
_____

Step 2: Where Is My Customer
Based on your itinerary, where is
your ideal customer spending time online?

Step 3: What to Pack
What are your SMART goals?
1.
2.
3. Big WHY
_____
_____

4. Your Marketing Story:

Step 4: How to Pack
Your Communication Style
KISS: Develop written content
Questions:_____
_____
Images:_____
_____
Themes:_____
_____

Step 5: How to Travel
Delivery: Practice styles
Time Management; Set calendar and
time allotments.

Bonus Itineraries
Advertising
Curation

You began planning your trip by identifying which so-cial media destinations make the most sense for you to visit based on your particular business. As you learned in the In-troduction, there are three itineraries to choose from, and one best fits your business. You can choose to add a second and even third itinerary as part of your MAP. You can even scale down your trip and plan to visit only one social media site, then ramp up your schedule as you become more com-fortable and familiar with the landscape.

Here's a brief summary of the three itineraries, to refresh your memory. On The Street is the itinerary for B2C busi-nesses, those establishments that are primarily business-to-consumer oriented. This would include storefronts, retail es-tablishments, and service providers, such as insurance agents and financial planners who deal with individual consumers. The Enterprise itinerary caters to B2B businesses and is for individuals who provide goods and services primarily to other businesses rather than directly to the end consumer. The third itinerary is Crossroads, for those who have customers in both B2C and B2B worlds. This tour is a perfect addition to a completed On The Street or Enterprise trip when you're ready to branch out and see more sights online.

The graphic below displays how the three social media itineraries fit together.

An On The Street trip focuses on Facebook and Pinterest as the best destinations to market your business. An Enterprise trip focuses on Twitter and LinkedIn as the best destinations to find ideal clients. A Crossroads trip, at the intersection of B2C and B2B, focuses on Google Plus and YouTube as the most effective destinations. Think about each of these itineraries in relation to your business, and then choose which one you want to begin with.

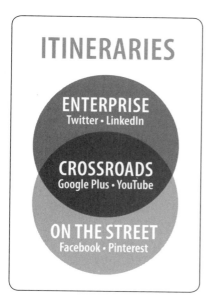

Does the fact that I have organized our six destinations into three separate tours mean that if you run a B2C business, you shouldn't use Twitter and LinkedIn, or vice versa for a B2B business with Facebook and Pinterest? *Absolutely not!* Your ultimate goal is to visit all six destinations and drive traffic to your business. But when you're starting from scratch you need a way to begin your strategy and avoid being overwhelmed. Too often even savvy boomers attempt to visit all six social media sites at the start, only to burn out before they reap any real reward. These three itineraries are my suggestions for how to begin you tour to avoid burnout, but they're no hard and fast rules.

Build Your MAP

Let's get down to it and build your social media MAP for navigating the digital highway. To get everything down on paper, we need to recap the previous chapters and finalize your decisions and research. Go to www.boomersultimateguidebooks.com (www.thebugbooks.com is a shortcut) for free worksheet downloads to help you complete each step of building your MAP. I ask that you share your name and email address with me to receive these helpful downloads.

Step 1 – Who Is My Customer

Identify your ideal customer. Make one or more representative models of individuals who are ideal prospects; we call these customer personas. You will need to identify as many characteristics as possible to develop each type of prospect into a fully formed person. If there are real customers or clients you wish you had more of, you can build models based on them. Try to answer the following questions and any other questions that you know are appropriate for your business. Granted, not all questions matter for every business niche, but it's best to be as specific as possible. Do this for as many varying types of prospects you want as customers in your business. At the very least, if appropriate, have one male and one female model.

♦ Typical demographics: sex, age range, ethnicity, educational level

- Family life: married, single, divorced, widowed, committed, lives in city, lives in suburbs, has children or not, lives with children or not, ages and sex of children

- Work life: employed, self-employed, business owner, business professional, service provider, travels to work, travels for work, works from home, strictly nine-to-five or non-traditional work schedule

- Lifestyle: lots of family time, lots of time devoted to work, enjoys travel, is building a business, participates in philanthropies, exercises, has hobbies and what hobbies, is religious or not, has extended family responsibilities or not, wears designer clothes, always dresses casually, drives a Prius, drives a Mercedes, drives an SUV

I think you get the picture. Create the ideal prospect for your business. This will help you determine how to speak to your prospects and what to say as we begin to pack for the trip for your chosen itinerary. Also, don't be surprised if at least one of your ideal models resembles . . . you.

☛ Hubspot, a noted marketing automation service, published a great article titled "100 Questions to Ask Yourself When Creating a Buyer Persona" at http://blog.hubspot.com/marketing/buyer-persona-100-questions. Read it and follow the instructions to gain insight into completing Step 1: Who Is My Customer.

Step 2 – Where Is My Customer

In Chapter 4 you created a picture in your mind of who frequents each of the six social media destinations. When you know who your customer is you can choose what itinerary you intend to focus on – On The Street, Enterprise, or Crossroads. Make sure you have a keen understanding of where your ideal prospects hang out and when they'll be accessible during your travels. Choose your destination accordingly, confident that your prospects are more likely to be visiting your chosen destinations and available for conversations. You're now ready to start packing for the trip.

⊗ I've told you to choose an Itinerary based on the type of business you're marketing – B2C or B2B. If you're building a MAP using the Enterprise itinerary for B2B business, and your ideal client is a woman between the ages of 25 and 35 years, LinkedIn and Twitter are still great social media destinations to travel, and she'll be there for you to meet. You also know that Pinterest is full of your ideal customers, even though Pinterest is on the B2C-focused On The Street itinerary. You know your business and customer personas better than anyone. Feel empowered to choose which social media sites to visit based on your knowledge of your business. In this example, there's nothing wrong with customizing your trip by choosing to use LinkedIn and Pinterest if those destinations uniquely suit your marketing objectives.

Step 3: What to Pack

Here's where you'll use the five steps for crafting the right message from Chapter 5: Understanding the Language of Social Media. This will help you pack the right content, said in a way that everyone can understand. You have discovered and defined your ideal prospect, and you know where they tend to hang out in social media. Now define your goals for using social media to market your business. Why are you looking to social media to create business growth?

Write down your goals. It's like making a list of all the places you want to visit while on your trip. Remember, a goal might be to drive traffic to your website, to build awareness for your brand or specific product or service, to position your business or yourself as a thought leader in the industry, or to create a movement that sustains your big WHY (see below). All goals are valid. Write down at least two distinct and tangible goals.

⭐ Goals are no good unless they're tangible. Here are five criteria that leadership expert and author Michael Hyatt says a good goal must have. He calls them SMART goals because they're:

1. **Specific:** Your goals must identify exactly what you want to accomplish with specificity. Bad: Start a Twitter account. Good: Use Twitter to increase traffic to our website.

2. **Measurable:** You want to know with certainty that you have hit the goal, so quantify it. Bad: Increase Twitter followers every month. Good: Increase Twitter followers by 500 every month.

3. **Actionable:** Every goal should start with an action verb rather than a to-be verb. Bad: Have new tweets every day. Good: Tweet new content five to seven times daily.

4. **Realistic:** Big goals are great and can stretch you, but you must also be realistic. Use common sense to define a goal that stretches but doesn't overwhelm you or set you up to fail. Bad: Have one million Twitter followers in six months. Good: Increase Twitter followers by 500 every month for six months, then increase 5 percent per week to 10,000 followers.

5. **Time-bound:** You need to associate a due date for the goal, otherwise it's a dream. Bad: Build Twitter to 10,000 followers. Good: Build Twitter to 10,000 followers in six months.

I mentioned your big WHY, but what does that mean exactly? Your big WHY is your *raison d'être,* or the reason for you being in business. You've chosen to start, run, or make a living in this particular business, and you need to define your reasons for doing so in writing. Don't get lame and say, "Because I want to help people," or even worse, "Because I want to make money." Making money is not enough of a goal to get you to start a business, and everyone wants to help people! Be specific.

- "Because I want to help people become financially free of debt," said the financial advisor.

- "Because I want to help people be free from pain," said the chiropractor.

- "Because I want to help people build the home of their dreams," said the architect.

- "Because I want to help people discover the sumptuous foods of my heritage," said the chef.

♦ "Because I want to help people build more profitable businesses so we can heal the economy," said me.

Get it? Put your big WHY down on paper.

☛ Your big WHY is my term for what Simon Sinek writes about in his wonderful book, *Start With Why*. Sinek teaches a concept called The Golden Circle, which defines how every organization functions on three levels – what we do, how we do it, and why we do it. Most of us define our businesses by what we do, and then we move on to how we do it, and hope that we do it differently from the competition. Marketers call this the USP, or unique selling proposition. Sinek goes on to say that most organizations never contemplate why they do it. Knowing why is what separates the mega-successful from the rest of the pack. The best way for you to understand how to define your big WHY is to watch Sinek's excellent TED talk, where he lays out the entire concept with examples that you're familiar with. Watch his 18-minute talk. It's well worth your time to get this part right. Go to www.TED.com and search for Simon Sinek. The talk was delivered in 2009 at TEDx Puget Sound and is titled, "How great leaders inspire action."

Now you know who your ideal prospects are, where they tend to be on the social media sites, why your business exists in a grand sense, and what goals you want to accomplish by engaging in social media to build your business. The next step in packing for this journey is to develop your marketing story.

Your marketing story, the story of your big WHY, is going to travel with you everywhere you go. Your marketing story could be about case studies of real clients and customers. Sharing how your business has succeeded at helping people will be memorable. Being memorable is a key feature of using social media successfully. Jot down a few case studies that explain your big WHY and showcase how you do that voodoo that you do so well.

If your business is newer, find case studies of existing businesses that have accomplished exactly what you intend to do. Don't steal case studies, but share the concept and what makes your business different. You can also write down case studies of your big WHY when you worked for another company, but don't imply that your new business is responsible for the results. You can even explain how you'll improve results now that you're at the wheel.

Try to identify a typical case study for each ideal prospect model you created during Step 1. Write down some examples specific to your business, and voilà! Your marketing story is born.

Step 4 – How to Pack

We're getting close now. Can you feel it? You know who your ideal prospects are, where they congregate, what your marketing story is, your big WHY for being in business, and the reason you have chosen social media as a method of delivering your marketing story. How to pack that story and bring it with you to each destination is where we use the communication concepts from Chapter 6.

In that chapter you learned the four styles of communication. You have a strong grasp on the suitcase that we've filled with content messages for your business, so you should have an idea of how you want to package your marketing story. Either your personal communication style fits your business brand or it doesn't, but your business definitely has a voice. Use that voice to communicate the information you want to share at each social media destination on your MAP.

Review the KISS principle and develop written content to share at each destination, following examples from Chapter 5. There's no need to reinvent the wheel every week or month. Develop themes and styles of questions, or types of statements that share your marketing story. You can recycle some of them periodically; others will be time-sensitive to the season, date, or current news. At all times remember to stay accessible, transparent, and consistent with both your story and frequency of sharing. This will create influence among your prospects, customers, clients, and fans at each destination.

Step 5 – How to Travel

Chapter 7: Transporting Content and Time Management gave you an overview of the three basic methods of delivering your marketing message. When you start out on this journey, visit social media destinations in person. It will give you a better understanding of how they work, what the people there expect from you as a citizen of the community, and whether your marketing story is resonating with them. Visiting in person is like walking around the community and getting to know it at the ground level, just as you might when you travel to a new destination and get settled in, walking the streets a few blocks in every direction from your hotel. Once you think you have a good grasp from walking, you can move on to different modes of transport.

Automation is less time-consuming, like flying, but you can't experience the ground-level view, and the people on the ground will never get to know you. A blend of in-person visits and automation is a bit more like driving. It saves time, but you still get the benefit of a ground-level view of the landscape. You can make a pit stop for some local conversation and then move on. For social media success, this blend of in-person visits with automated postings is your best option.

Of course your method of transport will impact your arrival time. Time management is a key factor in this whole endeavor. Traveling the digital highway of social media has a tendency to suck time out of your schedule in an insidious way. That's why it's critical to go through the steps I outlined in each chapter to plan your whole trip. Otherwise you may find social media frustrating, overwhelming, or downright disappointing. It's better to approach it as you would any other process in your business. Gather all your facts, apply best practices, and track your results.

Adapt my suggested daily and weekly schedules for a timed approach to implementing your strategy on your chosen itinerary. Block time in your calendar daily for working your social media MAP. Set up a spreadsheet for tracking results.

This brings me to some extras that you should know. Keep these in the back of your mind so that, when you're ready, you can upgrade your social media travel, become more sophisticated, and reap greater rewards.

Bonus Itineraries

Here are some bonus itineraries to help you get the most from each social media destination on your MAP.

Advertising: Both Facebook and Twitter have advertising platforms you can take advantage of to generate more traffic. Twitter allows you to promote chosen tweets. Facebook has an entire advertising program, which is often re-ferred to as pay-per-click or PPC, that many marketers swear rivals Google AdWords. On Facebook you can create images, tightly target demographics, and manage your ad spend to a great degree. This is definitely worth keeping in mind if your budget permits. Twitter is less useful, but it seems to get good traction for the Fortune 500. It's worth keeping an eye on and even trying on a smaller budget.

Curation: This is the term for gathering, accumulating, or mining content to share with the audience you build. As I mentioned before, it's a good idea to sign up for free daily, weekly, or monthly emails and digital newsletters from au-thorities in your industry. Their correspondence, delivered to your email address on a regular schedule, is a good source of content that your ideal prospects may find interesting and useful. There's no need for you to do all the searching if an industry leader, with a bigger budget, is already doing it for you. You can piggyback on what they're sharing and save your efforts for other things. Another way to reduce your workload is to subscribe to the blogs of industry leaders you enjoy reading. When you subscribe, you receive an email to your inbox every time a new blog post publishes. Then you can flag the article and put it in your content rotation.

What You Need to Know

♦   The process of developing a MAP for your business to use social media will weed out 99.9 percent of the errors you're likely to make if you don't have a plan, saving you time and money.

♦   You need to set tangible goals for this MAP that follow the SMART criteria.

♦   Why are you in business? The answer to this question can be the difference between limited success and stardom.

♦   When you have the budget, advertising on social media sites is economical and jumpstarts profitability.

CHAPTER TEN

* * * * *

Hit the Road

I can't change the direction of the wind, but I can adjust my sails to always reach my destination.

~ JIMMY DEAN

AND THERE YOU HAVE IT – the why and how of using social media to grow your business. Like the automobile, telephone, and television, some inventions change our lives forever. The Internet is one of those inventions. As with all new inventions, it's a blessing and a curse. The bottom line is, it's not going away.

The Internet has given us countless opportunities to connect to each other, but it comes at a cost. The way we communicate has changed dramatically and continues to change. Each generation engages differently with this new technology, creating an ever-widening gap. Gone are the days when you could count on everyone speaking the same language, verbally and non-verbally.

There's not always a linear path from your business to your customer. Now you have several meandering, intersecting paths where you can leave little bits of communication, trying to catch the attention of as many ideal prospects as possible in the hopes of leading them to your door. It's certainly not the most efficient way to communicate, but it can be effective when you understand how the virtual world works.

For us boomers it's been a strange experience to engage online at social media websites, with their multitude of messages formed in words, images, audio, and video. We are the generation that has seen tremendous change in the world in every aspect of life. Why should business communication be any different?

There are dozens of social media websites available to you, but I like to concentrate on those that are likely to bring you big results fast. That's why I suggest that you start this journey by looking at the six major stops in social media: Facebook, Twitter, LinkedIn, Pinterest, Google Plus, and YouTube. You can check out other sites once you get a handle on the whole process.

What to share when you engage with potential customers on social media can be a big pitfall. But now you know that communication is a multi-point conversation online, not a push-out with an advertisement for your message. Pushing out is like screaming, "Me, me, me!" at every turn. No one is interested in you, you, you for long if that's all you talk about.

We navigated through what to share online with your fans and followers. The content, or messages, that you pack to take with you on your journey will build relationships, not just make a sale.

In any communication, how you say it is as important as what you say. Remember, we all communicate through our own personal filters that we've spent a lifetime developing.

Being accessible, transparent, and consistent in the messages you send to potential customers will go a long way toward being heard and understood. If you want your message to resonate, knowing how to pack the content matters as much as the content itself.

You are a busy business owner running your enterprise every day. Whether you own the business, or you're responsible for your own personal profit and loss within a larger company, it's up to you to develop business and increase profits. How can you afford to add social media marketing efforts to your already over-loaded work schedule? That's why we went through various ways to deliver your content and considered time-management options that will keep you from feeling overwhelmed. Social media doesn't have to be time consuming to work. And to be highly successful you really need to add social media to your marketing mix.

What Now?

Now you have the tools to create a map, or rather MAP, to get you where you want and need to go. The first thing you need to do now? Determine what you want to accomplish by using social media in your business. Are you looking to increase awareness and build your reputation? Do you want the phone to ring 20 percent more often? Would having 15 percent more walk-ins do the trick? Maybe you want to start selling your products online as well as off. Perhaps you need to establish your brand in the marketplace or establish yourself as a thought leader in your industry. Every business is going to have different goals and reasons for marketing. Decide what you want; then start the journey in the order I've outlined for you.

Go online and download the free resources I've collected to help you build your MAP. They're waiting for you at www.boomersultimateguidebooks.com – worksheets, instructional videos, and more suggested resources that can help you succeed spectacularly.

Social media success stories are everywhere, and aren't just limited to big brands. Take WakeMed Health and Hospitals, for example. In Raleigh, North Carolina, WakeMed shared a time-lapse video taken from the hospital's helipad of a tornado that passed through the area. The tornado was a non-medical story, but it was a story directly related to the community that WakeMed is an integral part of and serves daily. The local newspaper praised WakeMed for the video, and it became one of the hospital's top blog posts. WakeMed showed that they're part of the community and paying attention to what's going on beyond their specific mission. It was a simple but effective strategy.

Listen to this success story on LinkedIn. A Morgan Stanley financial advisor actively participated in groups for small business CEOs, where he shared relevant content and established himself as an expert in small business. When he determined that he had reached a certain level of trust with an individual, he asked for a personal connection. One of those connections led to a $70 million account.[1]

Here's another good one. Is your niche very tight, very specific? So is Geoff Tucker's. He's an equine dentist with a regional service. He used his Facebook account to build new relationships, post videos, share blog posts, and expand his reach. He credits his Facebook and Twitter feeds for helping him win appearances on related horse-centric media outlets. In one year Facebook alone generated 100 new leads, 10–15 new customers, and an international reach.[2]

How about specific products like this one? SteelMaster makes prefabricated steel buildings. They developed a social media strategy on Facebook that let customers share photographs of their steel buildings in various uses. Sharing those uses opened up opportunities for SteelMaster in vertical markets that previously were unavailable to them.[3] When potential customers see your product in use by friends and colleagues, it triggers ideas and new opportunities for you. It also scales your efforts, saving you time.

Your MAP can be the next social media success story that mainstream media outlets herald as genius. You have the knowledge now. I told you it's not rocket science.

Plan the work and work the plan. Measure your successes again and again. You are great at what you do, and what you have chosen for your life's work matters. That's why it's so important for you to find ways to share it with more people. Let your MAP be your guide. Grow your business, help more people, make a difference, and prosper.

I look forward to seeing you on the open roads – of the digital highway.

PART THREE

♦ ♦ ♦ ♦ ♦

Appendices

APPENDIX A

• • • • •

Setting Up Your Social Media Accounts

I N THIS SECTION you'll find written instructions for creating accounts at each of our six social media destinations. Keep in mind that these sites are continually striving to improve the user experience. That means the step-by-step processes described in this chapter will change slightly every so often. The fundamentals won't change, but you may find that what's now a blue button changes to red, or a link that was in the upper right hand corner has moved to the lower middle of the page.

For that reason I suggest you go to www.boomersultimateguidebooks.com (or take the shortcut at www.thebugbooks.com), where you can download a Quick Start version of this Appendix in its most up-to-date form. Plus, the online version has screen shot images and examples to follow that you'll find helpful. You'll also appreciate the graphic examples and image sizes for profile pictures, cover photos, and more. All I ask is that you trust me with your name and email address on the opt-in form, and I'll set my smarty pants email system to send you the download automatically, 24/7/365.

Now let's start setting up those profiles!

 # Facebook

If On The Street is your first itinerary, Facebook is in your future. Follow these step-by-step instructions to successfully set up an account. While you're there, Like my page at www. facebook.com/kalynn.amadio and leave me a comment.

❶ Go to https://www.facebook.com/business/build/ and click **Create Page** on the upper left to get started. Facebook will ask you to log in. This is where you'll need to enter an email address and password to open a new account. Your business page will be separate from your personal profile. Only you will know that they're connected; visitors to your page will not know that you created the page.

    If you already have a personal Facebook profile, log in and then scroll down the left-hand side to **Pages** > **Create Page**. Both methods lead you to a webpage titled "Create a Page."

❷ Here you'll choose a page type that correlates best with your business. Choosing **Local Business** or **Place** is best if you have a physical location for your business, since Facebook will ask you to provide an address with this option. **Company, Organization** or **Institution** is a good option for other types of businesses, including online companies. A **Brand** or **Product** page is dedicated to an individual brand or product. If you are the brand, such as an author, artist, or public figure, choose **Artist, Band** or **Public Figure**. Non-profits fall under **Cause or Community**, and **Entertainment** pertains to movies, books, fictional characters, TV or radio stations, music, or art. Each choice typically has a drop-down menu where Facebook asks you to Choose a Category. You can look through these before making a decision if you're in doubt.

③ Click Facebook Pages Terms to find out Facebook's policies on naming, advertising, and other important aspects of using your Facebook page. Although terms of service are not a fun or engaging part of social media, it's a good idea to familiarize yourself with them. Facebook pages terms are not long.

④ To continue you must agree to these terms by clicking on the square next to I Agree to Facebook Pages Terms. After accepting the terms you can click the blue box that says Get Started to begin making your page.

⑤ Now Facebook will take you through four steps for setting up your page. You may skip any of the steps that you're not ready to complete, but note that each step is important in creating a complete page that's informative and professional.

Page Setup Step 1 – About

In this section you have space to describe your business, connect your page to a website, and choose an address for your Facebook page.

- Your description will be important for search engines, so be sure to include important keywords about your products, services, and location. Keep your description short. It's necessary to write a description before continuing to create your page.

- You can add any website you own to your Facebook page, including webpages, blogs, and other social media profiles. If you want to add more than one website to your page simply click Add Another Site.

- Choose a web address for your Facebook page, and be aware that this address can only be changed once after your page is made (see about the importance of having a vanity URL in Chapter 5. After completing all the information that you can in this step click Save Info.

Page Setup Step 2 – Profile Picture
Many businesses use their logo as the profile picture on their Facebook page. Facebook provides a square space for profile pictures, so make sure your image is properly formatted so that it won't look distorted (see account setup step 7 below). You may skip this step if you don't have an image ready, but it's important to go back and add one. You'll likely use the same square profile image on every social media profile you create.

Page Setup Step 3 – Add to Favorites
Here all you have to do is click the green button that says Add to Favorites to add the page to the favorites section of your personal account. This will make it easy to access the page from your personal profile. You can skip this step if you want to.

Page Setup Step 4 – Preferred Page Audience
In this step you have the ability to pay Facebook for advertising. Facebook will show your ad to users in the sidebar of their profile. You can choose to Add Payment Method without actually paying for adver-

tisements yet, or skip this step altogether if you think you want to develop your page more before paying for advertising. A paid Like campaign is a great way to get things started and is very cost effective.

6 After you complete these four steps Facebook will bring you to the **Admin Panel** for your brand new Facebook page! From here you should add a cover photo and tabs and start posting content. Post ten to twelve pieces of content, then invite Facebook friends and email contacts to Like your page. Avoid asking people to Like a page that's empty of content.

7 Here are the suggested sizes, width × height in pixels (px), of images you can use on Facebook. The profile image and cover photo have a fixed relationship with each other than can be fun to play with. Check the **Quick Start** guide for examples. Knowing this can help you do some clever things with the two images. The profile photo is 160 x 160 pixels and the cover photo is 851 x 315 pixels. The recommended size of post images you share is 1,200 × 630 pixels. For examples and the free *Quick Start* guide, go to www.boomersultimateguide-books.com (www.thebugbooks.com) to download.

Twitter

Twitter is a cornerstone of the Enterprise itinerary. It's also my favorite social media website, where you'll most likely find me hanging out. Follow me @kalynnamadio and follow The Boomer's Ultimate Guide brand from The Boomer Gal (that's me!) @BoomersUltimate.

❶ Go to http://www.twitter.com to create a profile.

❷ Add your name, or the name of your business, and an email address in the box that says New to Twitter? Sign up. Choose a secure password and click the yellow button that says Sign up for Twitter to get started.

❸ On the next screen check your information to make sure that it's correct. Twitter may suggest a username that will appear under Choose your username; feel free to change this. In fact, you should change it based on the vanity URL you're using. Remember, it's important to be consistent across all social media platforms. You'll actually be able to change your username at any time, but once you start getting followers you may not want to, so decide on a vanity URL that you can use on the majority of social media websites.

❹ Read through Twitter's Terms of Service and then click the Sign Up button at the bottom of the page.

❺ Now you have a new Twitter account. Twitter will walk you through a six-step setup process. It'll ask you questions and make suggestions for accounts you might want to follow.

❻ Twitter will suggest ways to build your timeline. You'll again see suggestions for accounts you may want to follow. You can skip any of these steps by clicking on the Skip this step for now link when it's available.

❼ On step four Twitter will allow you to upload a profile picture and header photo. Most businesses use their logo as a profile picture. Profile photos are almost always square. If your logo isn't square, make sure it's properly formatted so that it won't look distorted.

⑧ On your profile page click the Edit profile button on the right and fill out your bio. You can also change the cover photo or profile image here. Be aware that you only have 160 characters for your bio. To cover everything avoid writing in full sentences here. You can include keywords and hashtags in your bio.

⑨ Twitter will send an email to the address you used to sign up. When you confirm the email address your account will be complete and you can access all of Twitter's features.

⑩ Twitter image sizes as of 2015: Here are the sizes of images for Twitter, width × height in pixels (px). Profile image is 400 × 400 pixels. Header image is 1500 × 500 pixels. Newsfeed images should ideally be 440 × 220 pixels. For visual examples go to www.boomersultimateguidebooks.com (or take the shortcut www.thebugbooks.com) and download the free *Quick Start* guide.

LinkedIn

LinkedIn is the second cornerstone of an Enterprise itinerary. It's the most professional of the social media websites and a must for anyone who's in business or looking for a job (LinkedIn is the number one recruiting tool of Fortune 100 companies).

① Go to http://www.linkedin.com to create a personal profile.

② Enter your first and last name, an email address, and a secure password. Click the yellow Join now button to get started.

❸ LinkedIn will then take you through the steps of creating a profile. Start by entering your country, ZIP code, employment status, job title, and company in the designated boxes. Then click the blue Create my profile button.

❹ LinkedIn will suggest some people for you to follow, including well-known business leaders and contacts from your email account(s).

❺ By clicking the Profile tab at the top of the screen you can choose Edit Profile, where you can upload a profile picture and background photo and add information about yourself, your business, previous places of employment, education, volunteering experience, languages spoken, honors and awards, projects, patents you hold, test scores, publications you've been in, certifications, personal details, outside interests, and philanthropies. Your profile page is a very thorough resume.

❻ Before you can list your business with LinkedIn, your personal profile must have some connections, be at intermediate or all-star strength (your profile page will tell you its strength, which is increased the more fully you fill out your profile), and list your company in your personal experience.

❼ Your LinkedIn profile image has a minimum size of 200 × 200 pixels and a maximum size of 500 × 500 pixels. The background photo recommended size is 1400 × 425 pixels, width × height. When you build a business page on LinkedIn, the standard logo size is 100 × 60 pixels. The square logo is 50 × 50 pixels. The business can have a dedicated Career Page. The Career Page cover image

is 970 × 240 pixels. For visual examples go to www.
boomersultimateguidebooks.com (www.thebugbooks.
com) and download the free *Quick Start* guide.

 # Pinterest

Pinterest is the second half of the On The Street itinerary.
Pinterest is an image-based social media website and works
well for B2C, direct-to-consumer businesses. Clever B2B firms
have used Pinterest successfully as well; I include examples of
both in the free *Quick Start* guide available at www.boomer-
sultimateguidebooks.com (take the shortcut at www.thebug-
books.com). While you're there, follow me at www.pinterest.
com/kalynnamadio and check out some of my pin boards.

① Go to http://www.pinterest.com to set up your account.

② You can sign up with your Facebook login, or with your
email address. If you don't have a Facebook account
yet, clicking the Log In button will take you to a second
login screen that offers Facebook, Google Plus, or
Twitter as alternate login methods.

   To open a business account, go to http://business.
pinterest.com or click the Are you a business? Get
started here link just beneath the Password box.
Click the Join as a business button. The new screen
will ask for an email address, password, business name,
business type, and your website address.

③ Pinterest will walk you through a short tutorial explain-
ing what pins are and how you can best use the site. The
words at Pinterest that you'll see most often are *pin* or
pins and board. Pinterest is a virtual corkboard where

you pin images digitally. When you post to Pinterest either from your computer files or a link from the Internet, it's called a pin and you attach it to a board you've created. You can create as many boards as you like. Each board will have a title, preferably with a keyword.

❹ You can edit your profile any time by clicking on your name at the top right corner of the screen. Click the Edit profile button to make changes.

❺ Your profile page has a menu with options to navigate to your boards, pins, likes, followers, or following. These options will populate as you begin to use the site. To access additional functions, click the gear symbol next to the Edit profile button and a drop-down menu will appear.

❻ When you set up your account, Pinterest will suggest people or brands to follow to get you started. The pins from every person or company you follow will populate your Pinterest news feed. To get to the news feed, click the Pinterest logo (P) in the upper left-hand corner beside the search bar. Use the search bar to research thought leaders and brands that you would like to follow.

❼ The Pinterest profile image is 165 × 165 pixels. The background photo recommended size is 1400 × 425 pixels, width × height. Pinterest limits the width of pinned images but not length; image width of a pin is 236 pixels. Pinterest will scale down images to this width for the newsfeed. Your pin boards have a main image display that's 222 × 150 pixels, width × height. The smaller thumbnail image on your board will be 55 × 55 pixels. For visual examples, go to www.

boomersultimateguidebooks.com (www.thebugbooks. com) and download the free Quick Start guide.

 # Google Plus

Google Plus is one half of the dynamic Crossroads itinerary duo. Google Plus, or G+, is a good platform to add on when you feel that you have your first itinerary well under control. It's also a good social media website to use when your business straddles the fence between B2C and B2B. Unless your business is new, chances are it already has a business page on G+. Search Google Plus for your business to see if it already exists in the directory, and if it does, claim it. Feel free to reach out and follow me at www.plus.google. com/+KalynnAmadio.

① Go to https://plus.google.com to create a personal profile.

② If you already have a Gmail or Google account for your business, log in using that information. If not, you'll be prompted to open a personal Google account. Click the **Create An Account** or **Add Account** link/button on the page. Fill out your information. Use your real name, not a fictitious persona. Google is a stickler that real humans use their products. They want you to be transparent in terms of who you are and where you are.

③ Signing in will automatically take you to your profile, where you can find people you know using your existing email contacts. You can skip any steps by clicking on **Continue** at the bottom of the page.

④ After creating an account, notice that the upper right-hand corner of your page will show **+YourFirstName** rather than the default +You. Clicking on that link will take you to your Google Plus page.

⑤ Your menu options will appear along the left-hand side of the page. Go to the Profile tab and hover your mouse over different parts of your profile to make changes. You can also edit your profile by clicking the About tab at the top of your profile page.

⑥ Google requires you to have a personal account before you create a local business page or brand page. To get your business on Google Plus use the Google My Business program https://www.google.com/business and click the Get on Google button.

⑦ Google will take you to a search box. This is where you can search to see if Google already has your business listed. Check your current mailing address and former addresses to see if they're in the directory. You don't want to create a duplicate business listing. If your business comes up, click its link and follow the steps to claim it. If you can't find any record of your business, follow the steps to add it. When you're done your business will have a Google Plus page just like your personal profile page. It even functions the same way; businesses can use G+ the same way individuals do.

⑧ The Google Plus profile image has a recommended minimum size of 120×120 pixels and appears in a circle. The cover photo is 1080×608 pixels, width $\times$ height (the minimum cover photo size you can submit is 480×270 pixels and the maximum size is 2120×1192 pixels). These image sizes apply to personal profiles and business pages. Shared content images come in two sizes: 497 × 279 pixels minimum for images you upload and 150 × 150 pixels when the image is pulled in from an Internet link. For visual examples go to www.boomersultimateguidebooks.com (www.thebugbooks.com is your shortcut) and download the free *Quick Start* guide.

YouTube

YouTube is a video-based social media platform that finishes out the Crossroads itinerary. While several of our travel destinations can share video, YouTube is the only site that is exclusively video. YouTube is owned by Google and is an important part of their playground. You can reach my YouTube channel from Google Plus or take the shortcut http://bit.ly/kalynn-amadio-youtube.

❶ Go to www.youtube.com and click the Sign in button in the top right corner of the page. You'll be prompted to sign in to your Google account. In order to create a YouTube account you must have a Google account. If you already have a Google account skip to Step 4.

❷ If you don't have a Google account, return to the Google Plus section of this Appendix for instructions on signing up for one.

❸ Read and agree to the Terms of Service and Privacy Policy. When you create an account be sure that the user name you choose relates to your business, since this will be the username for your YouTube account (also called a YouTube channel). Use the vanity URL name you've chosen at other destinations so that your various social media accounts are consistent. Return to www.youtube.

com, click the Sign in button in the top right corner of the page, and sign in to your Google account.

④ You'll be asked to confirm your email address before you get full access to your account. YouTube will take you to a welcome page that suggests channels for you to subscribe to. You can skip this step by clicking on the Next button in the bottom left corner of the window. YouTube will automatically choose channels for you to subscribe to, and in this step you can either save them or uncheck those you're not interested in.

⑤ At YouTube.com, on the left-hand menu, click My Channel to get to your new page. YouTube will use the profile image associated with your Google account. There's also an area for a cover image. Your channel cover photo should be 2560 × 1440 pixels, width × height. Hover your mouse over the upper right hand corner of the cover photo area to reveal a pencil. Click it and that will give you choices to edit the cover photo and links from your Channel to your website or other social media profiles.

⑥ Click the Video Manager tab above the cover photo to get to your Channel dashboard area. On the left-hand menu are various options for configuring your account. On the My Channel page you can configure how your channel looks. Hover your mouse over the different sections and click to enter an edit mode. Play with the settings until you're familiar with them. Many of the functions won't make sense until you have videos uploaded to display. For visual examples, visit www. boomersultimateguidebooks.com (www.thebugbooks. com) and download the free *Quick Start* guide.

Marketing Action Plan Template

B Y ANSWERING THE FOLLOWING QUESTIONS you will build your roadmap that will guide your travel to any or all of the six destinations covered in this guide.

Destination

Where do you want to go and why (who do you expect to find there)? What actions will you need to take in choosing your destinations and itinerary?

- ◆ On the Street Itinerary (Facebook, Pinterest): For business-to-consumer (B2C) companies

- ◆ Enterprise Itinerary (Twitter, LinkedIn): For business-to-business (B2B) companies

- ◆ Crossroads Itinerary (Google Plus, YouTube): For companies that are both B2C and B2B

Language

What exactly are you going to talk about when you visit? What content should you leave behind after you've made initial contact with people and businesses so potential leads will remember you? What actions will you need to take to address each of the five plans for dealing with your content?

- Keep It Simple Stupid
- Keep It Social
- Tell A Story
- Make It Scalable
- Have a Social Media Strategy

Etiquette

How will you engage potential customers? What communication style will you adopt? What actions will you need to take to incorporate each of the four plans in your communications?

- Be Accessible
- Be Transparent
- Be Consistent
- Be Influential

Transportation

How will your content be delivered to the various social media destinations? What actions will you need to take to deliver it?

- Hand-deliver
- Automated delivery
- Blend of Both

Time Management

Which road will you travel on to deliver your content in a way that optimizes your personal time management? What actions will you need to take in choosing between the two roads?

- Do It Yourself Road
- Outsource Road

Frequency

How often should you share content? What are the best times? What actions will you need to take to schedule your sharing frequencies?

Metrics

How will you know whether your social media marketing activities are successful? What metrics will you use to measure success? What actions will you need to take to measure the success of your social media marketing activities?

Additional Resources

THE BOOMER'S ULTIMATE GUIDE TO SOCIAL MEDIA MARKETING is meant to be a starting point, a beginner's guide that can help you start using the tools of social media to build a thriving business. But there's much, much more outside these pages that can help you succeed with social media. Here's a brief list worth considering.

Keep in Touch

First you'll want to be on my mailing list. Visit www.The-BoomerGal.com and sign up for my email updates. I send you useful information, keep you informed on how changes to social media can impact your business, and cut through the clutter so you don't have to.

www.ACTLOCALmarketing.com
www.TheBoomerGal.com
www.boomersultimateguidebooks.com
(www.thebugbooks.com)

Social Media's Top 10 Blogs

Each year Social Media Examiner (a blog on my personal Top 10 list!) holds a contest where a panel of social media experts chooses from hundreds of blogs, which have been submitted to them by readers, to be chosen as the Best Of for that year. Over 600 blogs were submitted for the 2015 list. You'll also find it worth your while to visit www.SocialMediaExaminer.com to check out the blogs that were chosen as Best Of in past years. Below are the Top 10 Social Media Blogs for 2015, along with advice from me on how they might fit into your MAP.

1. **Buffer Social** – Buffer is a great social media automation tool. Their blog, one of my favorites, walks the walk by curating comprehensive content that's useful for beginners and experts. https://blog.bufferapp.com

2. **Grow** – This blog is by Mark W. Schaefer, who has written some great social media books too. He's a great resource on social media, and I follow him regularly. www.businessesgrow.com/blog/

3. **Jon Loomer** – Jon shares in-depth articles focused on Facebook. If you're building a MAP that includes an On The Street itinerary, check out his real-life examples and support graphics. www.JonLoomer.com

4. **Convince & Convert** – This blog shares the insights of a social media powerhouse, Jay Baer. Jay is well established in the field and delivers consistently great content. His podcast is good too. www.convinceandconvert.com

⑤ **Rebekah Radice** – A thought leader I follow on Twitter, she has an easy-to-read blog that gives marketing advice to newbie through intermediate-level users. www. rebekahradice.com/blog

⑥ **Socially Sorted** – This blog from down under has great visuals and headlines we can all learn from. www. sociallysorted.com.au/blog

⑦ **RazorSocial** – Ian Cleary provides no-nonsense, practical, and actionable articles to help you get more from your social media strategy. www.razorsocial.com/ blog

⑧ **Jenn's Trends** – This blog by Jenn Herman is something you'll want to check out. She focuses on Instagram for businesses. Instagram is a great add-on for the On The Street itinerary. Jenn's tips are geared for everyone, from novice to advanced users. www.jennstrends.com/blog

⑨ **Simply Measured** – Check out this blog for outstanding data and actual case studies. If you like to see nuts and bolts, this blog will help you understand how to apply real-life examples to your own MAP. www. simplymeasured.com/blog

⑩ **SocialBro** – This blog has high-quality posts focused on Twitter topics. It's worth checking out to find golden nuggets that you can absorb into your plan. www. socialbro.com/blog

Top 10 Business Books

Social media is but one aspect of running a thriving business. Here's my list of Top 10 Business Books that will help you and your business grow.

1. ***Influence: The Psychology of Persuasion*** by Robert Cialdini – It's a classic for a reason. I've spoken of this book often in my podcast.

2. ***Getting Things Done*** by David Allen – This book is another classic. It's about time management, which is key to using social media effectively and not getting sucked into the vortex.

3. ***Guerrilla Marketing*** by Jay Conrad Levinson – Okay, I keep picking classics, but building a strong foundation is crucial. This is a pivotal book about marketing a local business, and it continues to resonate. Once you've read these three classics you can check out the rest.

4. ***The Success Principles: How to Get from Where You Are to Where You Want to Be*** by Jack Canfield – More than a business book, it's a book on how to live your life. I refer to it often when there's some obstacle in my way that I need to get around.

5. ***Purple Cow*** by Seth Godin – All Seth's books are worth reading, but this is the one that will help you understand the importance of differentiation.

6. ***Think and Grow Rich*** by Napoleon Hill – Although the book was written in 1937, you'll be surprised by how fundamentally sound its precepts are today. Definitely worth a read, or two.

7 *The E-Myth: Why Most Small Businesses Don't Work and What to Do About It* by Michael Gerber – If your business relies on you to make it run, then you're doing something wrong.

8 *How the World Sees You: Discover Your Highest Value Through the Science of Fascination* by Sally Hogshead – This book will help you align marketing and leadership practices with your personality so that you don't spend time trying to be something you're not.

9 *Platform: Get Noticed in a Noisy World* by Michael Hyatt – The Internet has made our world very noisy. The more of us who use it to market, the harder it becomes to get noticed. This book will help you to understand the principles behind building a platform so your messages are heard.

10 *Shareology: How Sharing is Powering the Human Economy* by Bryan Kramer – I know it can sometimes feel wrong to give away your intellectual property on social media. This book helps explain why sharing what you know is powerful, and it will help you make what you share more valuable to others.

Favorite YouTube Channels

If you like to watch high-quality content from entrepreneurs and social-media-savvy business people, these channels will give you plenty to consume.

1. **Marie TV** by Marie Forleo – This is a favorite of mine. Marie offers excellent content with a new video every week.

2. **Jill Konrath** by Jill Konrath – She's a sought-after sales specialist and has great content on how to be a better sales person in a completely authentic way.

3. **Derek Halpern** by Derek Halpern – This guy fascinates me with his take on the entire marketing and sales process. He's young and immersed in the psychology behind why we make the decisions we do. Very valuable stuff.

4. **Brendon Burchard** by Brendon Burchard – An early mentor of mine, he taught me many life and business lessons. He's a consummate marketer and worth every minute you can spend with him.

5. **TED** – TED and TEDx talks are a surprisingly good place to find content. They can be hit or miss, but watching the top playlists is worth the time. Who knows, maybe I'll see you on one!

6. **Possibility Partners** by Ande Lyons – A lesser-known entrepreneur, Ande is a personal friend who really gets the whole "social" aspect of social media and does a great video podcast on YouTube using Google Plus Hangouts.

Top Digital Tools

I created a free PDF download with 41 of my favorite digital tools. It's called *Inside My Digital Toolbox: 41 Resources That Will Help You Grow A Thriving Business And Vibrant Life*, and you can get it by going to www.TheBoomerGal.com and signing up for my email list.

It's been a pleasure helping you, and I look forward to meeting you on the digital highway. Be sure to wave and say hello.

REFERENCES

♦ ♦ ♦ ♦ ♦

Introduction

1. eBiz, "Top 15 Most Popular Social Networking Websites," eBizMBA Guide, June 2015, http://www.ebizmba.com/articles/social-networking-websites.
2. Erik Qualman, "Social Media Video," November 20, 2012, http://www.youtube.com/watch?v=QUCfFcchw1w.
3. Katy Daniels, "Social Media Stats," Digital Buzz Blog, November 14, 2013, http://www.digitalbuzzblog.com/infographic-social-media-stats-2013.
4. Greg Sterling, "Nielson: More Time On Internet Through Smartphones Than PCs," Marketing Land, February 11, 2014, http://marketingland.com/nielsen-time-accessing-internet-smartphones-pcs-73683.

Chapter 1

1. Bret Peterson, "Stream Social Q1 2013: Facebook Active Usage Booms," Global Web Index, April 26, 2013, http://blog.globalwebindex.net/Stream-Social.
2. comScore, "55% of Social Networking Consumption Occurs on a Mobile Device," Marketing Charts, February 27, 2013, http://www.marketingcharts.com/online/55-of-social-networking-consumption-occurs-on-a-mobile-device-27327/.
3. Nielsen, "Emerging Trends in Mobile and What They Mean for Your Business," Nielsen, August 5, 2014, http://www.nielsen.com/us/en/insights/news/2014/emerging-trends-in-mobile-and-what-they-mean-for-your-business.html.
4. Philip Elmer-DeWitt, "Americans Spend 2:38 Hours a Day Glued to Their Tablets and Smartphones," Fortune, April 3, 2013, http://fortune.com/2013/04/03/report-americans-spend-238-hours-a-day-glued-to-their-tablets-and-smartphones/.
5. Mark Krantz, "Facebook Squeezes onto the Fortune 500," USA Today, May 6, 2013, http://www.usatoday.com/story/money/business/2013/05/06/facebook-fortune-500-2013/2139223/.
6. Emil Protalinski, "Facebook Passes 1.23 Billion Monthly Active Users, 945 Million Mobile Users, and 757 Million Daily Users, TNW News, January 29, 2014, http://thenextweb.com/facebook/2014/01/29/facebook-passes-1-23-billion-monthly-active-users-945-million-mobile-users-757-million-daily-users/.

7. Jeff Bullas, "21 Awesome Social Media Facts, Figures and Statistics for 2013," Yahoo Small Business, https://smallbusiness.yahoo.com/advisor/21-awesome-social-media-facts-figures-statistics-2013-231748416.html.

8. Sebastian Hedencrona, "Twitter Now the Fastest Growing Social Platform in the World," Global Web Index, January 28, 2013, http://blog.globalwebindex.net/twitter-now-the-fastest-growing-social-platform-in-the-world/.

9. YouTube, "Statistics," YouTube, http://www.youtube.com/yt/press/statistics.html.

10. Ibid.

11. GlobalWebIndex, "Stream Social: Quarterly Social Platforms Update, Q1 – 2013," Global Web Index via Slideshare, May 1, 2013, http://www.slideshare.net/globalwebindex/globalwebindex-stream-social-q1-2013-report-preview.

12. Ibid.

13. Wikipedia contributors, "History of Mobile Phones," Wikipedia, http://en.wikipedia.org/wiki/History_of_mobile_phones.

14. Ibid.

15. NPD Group, "PC Users Increasingly Turning to Smart Devices for Web Browsing, Facebook Access," Marketing Charts, February 11, 2013, http://www.marketingcharts.com/online/pc-users-increasingly-turning-to-smart-devices-for-web-browsing-facebook-access-26881/.

16. Mobithinking, "Global Mobile Statistics 2014 Home," mobiForge, June 13, 2014, http://mobiforge.com/research-analysis/global-mobile-statistics-2014-home-all-latest-stats-mobile-web-apps-marketing-advertising-subscriber.

17. Qualcomm, "Mobile Device, Cell Phone Statistics," Statistic Brain Research Institute, March 17, 2015, http://www.statisticbrain.com/mobile-device-cell-phone-statistics/.

18. Timothy Lemke, "Does Online Yellow Page Advertising Still Have Value?" Local Fresh, March 18, 2014, http://localfresh.biz/2014/03/online-yellow-page-advertising-still-value/.

Chapter 2

1. Kalynn Amadio, "Marketing Strategies for Smart Entrepreneurs – David Newman, Do It! Marketing," ACT LOCAL Marketing for Small Business, January 21, 2014, http://actlocalmarketing.com/marketing-strategies-for-smart-entrepreneurs/.

2. Erica Swallow, "5 Small Business Social Media Success Stories," Mashable, June 2, 2010, http://mashable.com/2010/06/02/small-business-social-media-success-stories/.

3. Connie Benson, "Social Media Wins: How Coconut Bliss Boosts Fan Engagement," Social Business Connection, September 23, 2012, http://en.community.dell.com/dell-groups/sbc/b/weblog/archive/2012/09/23/social-media-wins-how-coconut-bliss-boosts-fan-engagement.aspx.

4. Phil Mershon, "9 Small Business Social Media Success Stories," Social Media Examiner, January 18, 2012, http://www.socialmediaexaminer.com/9-small-business-social-media-success-stories/.

5. Jennifer Tribe, "3 B2B Case Studies That Prove the Power of Content Marketing," Clearprose Communications, January 30, 2014, http://www.clearprose.com/b2b-case-studies-prove-power-content-marketing/.

6. Arik Hanson, "3 B2B Social Media Case Studies and Why They Work," Communications Conversations, September 17, 2010, http://www.arikhanson.com/2010/09/17/3-b2b-social-media-case-studies-and-why-they-work/.

Chapter 4

1. Pew Research Center, "Social Networking Fact Sheet," January 2014, http://pewinternet.org/fact-sheets/social-networking-fact-sheet/.

2. Cooper Smith, "The Surprising Facts About Who Shops Online and on Mobile," Business Insider, February 23, 2015 , http://www.businessinsider.com/the-surprising-demographics-of-who-shops-online-and-on-mobile-2014-6.

3. Facebook, "Company Info," Facebook, 2015, https://newsroom.fb.com/Key-Facts.

4. Maeve Duggan and Aaron Smith, "Social Media Update 2013," Pew Research Center, December 30, 2013, http://www.pewinternet.org/2013/12/30/social-media-update-2013/.

5. IBM Global Services, "Leading through Connections: Insights from the IBM CEO Study, December 2012, IBM, http://www-935.ibm.com/services/us/en/c-suite/ceostudy2012/index.html.

6. Adobe, "The CMO's Guide to the 2014 Social Landscape," CMO., March 21, 2014, http://www.cmo.com/articles/2014/3/13/_2014_social_intro.html.

7. Sebastian Hedencrona, "Twitter Now the Fastest Growing Social Platform in the World," Global Web Index, January 28, 2013, http://blog.globalwebindex.net/twitter-now-the-fastest-growing-social-platform-in-the-world/.

8. LinkedIn, "LinkedIn," 2015, http://www.linkedin.com.

9. Ibid.

10. Reuters, "Pinterest Is Worth $2 Billion Because Its 25 Million Users Are Rich, Female, and Like to Spend," Business Insider, February 28, 2013, http://www.businessinsider.com/pinterest-is-worth-2-billion-because-its-25-million-users-are-rich-female-and-like-to-spend-2013-2.

11. Adobe, see reference 6.

12. Shuilpa Shree, "Social Media Statistics 2013: Facebook, Twitter, Google+, Instagram, Pinterest, and More!!!" Daze Info, January 10, 2013, http://www.dazeinfo.com/2013/01/10/social-media-statistics-2013-facts-figures-facebook-twitter/.

13. Alistair Barr, "Google's Social Network Sees 58% Jump in Users," USA Today, October 29, 2013, http://www.usatoday.com/story/tech/2013/10/29/google-plus/3296017/.

14. comScore, "comScore Releases March 2014 U.S. Search Engine Rankings," comScore, April 15, 2014, https://www.comscore.com/Insights/Press-Releases/2014/4/comScore-Releases-March-2014-U.S.-Search-Engine-Rankings.

15. "Search engine optimization," https://en.wikipedia.org/wiki/Search_engine_optimization.

16. Google, "YouTube Demographics," ThinkWithGoogle, http://www.thinkwithgoogle.com/products/youtube-demographics.html.

17. Jeff Bullas, "The Facts and Figures on YouTube in 2013," Jeff Bullas, 2013, http://www.jeffbullas.com/2013/02/11/the-facts-and-figures-on-youtube-in-2013-infographic/.

18. Diode Digital, "Online Video Statistics 2013," Diode Digital, May 22, 2013, http://www.youtube.com/watch?v=4sVv9CHsY40.

19. YouTube, "Statistics," YouTube, 2015, http://www.youtube.com/yt/press/statistics.html.

Chapter 5

1. Wikipedia contributors, "KISS Principle," Wikipedia, http://en.wikipedia.org/wiki/K.I.S.S.

2. Nick Brady, "Disruptive Communication," Razorfish Search, July 18, 2011, http://razorfishsearch.com/2011/07/18/disruptive-communication/#sthash.gMryJxma.Yo8Cg2iV.dpbs.

3. Gary Vaynerchuk, The Thank You Economy (2011).

4. Seth Godin, Permission Marketing: Turning Strangers into Friends and Friends into Customers, (1999).

5. Jonathan Gottschall, "Why Storytelling is the Ultimate Weapon," Fast Company, May 2, 2012, http://www.fastcocreate.com/1680581/why-storytelling-is-the-ultimate-weapon.

6. Helen Nesterenko, "7 Ways to Integrate More Brand Storytelling in Your Content Marketing Strategy," Social Media Today, June 26, 2013, http://socialmediatoday.com/helen-nesterenko/1560541/7-ways-integrate-more-brand-storytelling-your-content-marketing-strategy.

Miscellaneous References

- Sean D'Souza, "The 3 Core Elements of Good Storytelling (And Why Your Business Needs Them)," Copy Blogger, July 16, 2013, http://www.copyblogger.com/cinderella-content-marketing/?utm_source=buffer&utm_campaign=Buffer&utm_content=buffer0ebea&utm_medium=twitter.

- Brandon Yanofsky, "A Crash Course in Marketing with Stories," Copy Blogger, August 2, 2011, http://www.copyblogger.com/storytelling-marketing/.

- Susan Gunelius, "5 Secrets to Use Storytelling for Brand Marketing Success," Forbes, February 5, 2013, http://www.forbes.com/sites/work-in-progress/2013/02/05/5-secrets-to-using-storytelling-for-brand-marketing-success/.
- Chris Brogan, "Scaling Social Media," Chris Brogan, March 22, 2010, http://www.chrisbrogan.com/scaling-social-media/.
- Rosalia Cefalu, "Can a People-Centric Social Media Strategy Scale?" Hubspot, May 30, 2013, http://blog.hubspot.com/can-a-people-centric-social-media-strategy-scale.
- Phil Mershon, "9 Small Business Social Media Success Stories," Social Media Examiner, January 18, 2012, http://www.socialmedia-examiner.com/9-small-business-social-media-success-stories/.
- Sam Decker, "Three Key Principles to Maximize Your Converged Media Strategy," Duct Tape Marketing, October 3, 2013, http://www.ducttapemarketing.com/blog/?s=scaling+.
- Scott Gerber, "9 Key Elements Missing from Your Social Strategy," Mashable, July 2, 2013, http://mashable.com/2013/07/02/social-media-plan-missing/.
- Jay Baer, "Social Media Strategy in 8 Steps," Convince & Convert, http://www.convinceandconvert.com/social-media-strategy/social-media-strategy-in-8-steps/.
- Heidi Cohen, "How to Setup a Social Media Business Strategy," Social Media Examiner, June 26, 2013, http://www.socialmediaexaminer.com/how-to-setup-a-social-media-business-strategy/.
- Kalynn Amadio, "Writing Good Copy with Lisa Manyon," ACT LOCAL Marketing for Small Business: http://actlocalmarketing.com/writing-good-copy-lisa-manyon/.
- John Heywood, "John Heywood Quotes," BrainyQuote, http://www.brainyquote.com/quotes/quotes/j/johnheywoo158880.html.

Chapter 6

Miscellaneous References

- Sherrie Bourg Carter, "Are We Talking the Same Language? How Communication Styles Can Affect Relationships," Psychology Today, April 27, 2011, http://www.psychologytoday.com/blog/high-octane-women/201104/are-we-talking-the-same-language-how-communication-styles-can-affect-r.
- Courtney Ramirez, "How to Create a Social Media Guide for Your Brand," Maximize Social Business, July 23, 2013, http://maximizesocialbusiness.com/how-to-create-a-social-media-style-guide-for-your-brand-9544/.
- Matthew Latkiewicz, "How To: Pick the Right Social Media Engagement Style," Mashable, August 11, 2010, http://mashable.com/2010/08/11/customer-engagement-style/.

Chapter 7

1. Jennifer Van Grove, "3 Great Social Media Policies to Steal From," Mashable, October 2, 2009, http://mashable.com/2009/10/02/social-media-policy-examples/.
2. Corey Eridon, "5 Noteworthy Examples of Corporate Social Media Policies," Hubspot, December 14, 2011, http://blog.hubspot.com/blog/tabid/6307/bid/29441/5-Noteworthy-Examples-of-Corporate-Social-Media-Policies.aspx.

Miscellaneous References
- Tiffany Black, "How to Write a Social Media Policy, Inc., May 27, 2010, http://www.inc.com/guides/2010/05/writing-a-social-media-policy.html.
- Chris Boudreaux, "Social Media Policy Database," Social Media Governance, 2015, http://socialmediagovernance.com/policies.php.

Chapter 8

Miscellaneous References
- Leo Widrich, "5 Essential Social Media Metrics to Track and How to Improve Them," Buffer, April 16, 2013, http://blog.bufferapp.com/social-media-metrics-improve.
- Harry Gold, "14 Social Media ROI Metrics You Can Use Right Now!" ClickZ, December 18, 2012, http://www.clickz.com/clickz/column/2178428/14-social-media-roi-metrics.
- A.J. Kumar, "3 Social Media Metrics Your Business Should Track" Social Media Examiner, April 11, 2013, http://www.socialmediaexaminer.com/3-social-media-metrics-your-business-should-track/.

Chapter 10

1. Amy McIlwain, "Why Advisors Need to Get Social: 3 Social Media Success Stories to Convince You," Financial Social Media, August 29, 2013, http://financialsocialmedia.com/why-advisors-need-to-get-social-3-success-stories-that-will-convince-you/.
2. Rick Burnes, "5 Surprising Social Media Business Success Stories," Mashable, May 21, 2010, http://mashable.com/2010/05/21/surprising-social-media-business-success/.
3. Ibid.

INDEX

◆ ◆ ◆ ◆ ◆

ABOUT THE AUTHOR

✦ ✦ ✦ ✦ ✦

Kalynn Amadio – The Boomer Gal – is an author, speaker, and engineer, helping entrepreneurs over 50 who struggle with technology and feel like digital dinosaurs. She personally guides you across the technology bridge into the 21st century so you can build a thriving business and vibrant life. She is the host of *ACT LOCAL Marketing for Small Business* podcast and *The Boomer's Ultimate Guide Podcast,* both on iTunes. She is the author of "The Inner Entrepreneur," a chapter in *Messages that Matter* by Jill Lublin.

Kalynn speaks regularly in the New York City tri-state area on various aspects of online marketing. Her humorous and engaging "let's get it done" attitude has been featured on several business podcasts and radio shows where she shares her best secrets for digital marketing success.

As a Baby Boomer, online marketing consultant, engineer, lighting designer, Schnoodle owner, radio host, mom, and romance-novel-reading, third-degree black belt, Kalynn understands the busy life of a small business owner and tailors her guidance to help you make the best use of your time and talent while reaping the rewards of successful digital marketing.

www.ACTLOCALmarketing.com
www.TheBoomerGal.com
www.boomersultimateguidebooks.com
(www.thebugbooks.com)